WRITE ANGLES

A Collection of Poetry and Prose

WRITE ANGLES

A Collection of Poetry and Prose

Edited by The Spastics Society

HODDER AND STOUGHTON IN
ASSOCIATION WITH THE SPASTICS
SOCIETY

British Library Cataloguing in Publication Data
Write angles.
  1. English literature—20th century
  I. Spastics Society
  820.8'00914   PR1148

ISBN 0 340 36151 4

CONTENTS

EXPERIENCE

THE SEASONS

FOREWORD

I am delighted to be associated with the publication of WRITE ANGLES and hope that it is only the first collection of works by men and women who suffer from some form of physical disability.

Past winners include Christopher Nolan whose DAM-BURST OF DREAMS was published in 1981, David Swift, Lyn Berwick and Richard Gomm. This selection of past entries (the first to be published in this form) has created a high standard that will be hard to surpass. The pieces range from the highly amusing 'Oh 'L' It's Owen' to the truly moving 'Coda'.

The Spastics Society is hoping that with the successful publication of this book many new writers will now consider entering next year's competition thus raising standards even higher.

The Society sees this as another positive way of integrating into the community those people whose talents are not obvious to the naked eye. To that end I am proud to play a small part in the publication of WRITE ANGLES and have no doubt that it will survive in a commercial world because of its quality.

J<small>EFFREY</small> A<small>RCHER</small>

PREFACE

The first literary contest organised by The Spastics Society in 1970–71 was so successful that it became an annual event and entries were invited from people with any disability. It is now open to writers who have become disabled in adulthood as well as earlier in life.

Over the years many eminent people have given their time to judge the various entries and to attend the presentation of prizes; an occasion enjoyed by all.

The standard of writing has always been high. I have judged the poetry section each year and have been very interested in the diverse choice of subject material. Much of the work is contemplative but those poems concerning activities outside the writer's own experience show powerful imagination. I remember a particularly vivid poem about climbing a mountain by a young man who was unable to walk. The few people who write directly about their disabilities produce informative, thought-provoking work giving an insight into the positive side as well as the difficulties of handicap.

Several of the contestants have entered year after year and so become old friends although there is a restriction on the same people collecting all the prizes.

I am very pleased that the generosity of Jeffrey Archer in donating a year's public library lending right income has made it possible to collect together some of the contributions in this book. I am sure that the reader will agree that it is an anthology which deserves to stand alongside collections by better known writers.

LADY WILSON

PERCEPTION

A WONDROUS MOMENT

Dawn.
A rosebud sleeps, petals tightly furled;
Sepal fingers cupping it gently,
Protectingly,
Until,
Roused by the soft, warm flush of morning
A faint stirring signals its awakening.

Quietly I watch,
Fascinated, as, one by one
The sepals loose their hold;
Fall outward and down,
Folding over to form a pedestal
Upon which to display the ultimate glory
Of the rose – queen of the garden.

Slowly the bud expands,
With imperceptible speed pushing,
Pushing.
The vital urge to fulfil its destiny
Transcending all else.
See!
The tip is opening now.

Snap! – the minutest wisp of sound,
So clear and sharp I stare, amazed –
Joyously the first petal leaps away,
Revealing all the glowing loveliness
Of powdered carmine,
Velvet soft, delicately etched
Upon the purest gold.

Within this wondrous moment lies Eternity.

Nellie de Beaufort Saunders, 1980

THE HUMMING BIRD

A knot of dusty feathers
Pinned in a box of glass –
I saw it on a museum shelf
When, on a rainy afternoon,
I had an hour to pass.

The rain and city dust did fade
As, for a moment brief,
I saw a distant sparkling shore
And palms in young green leaf:
A radiant winged spirit there
Did dart and flash before his mate,
Pledging his love, his very self . . .

Alas, that this should be his fate!
He lies, at last,
With pins and glass,
In dust on the museum shelf.

But still upon that palmy shore
The winged spirit flies:
Not one, but hosts innumerable,
For beauty never dies.
And love endures, altho' it's pinned in boxes,
And re-creates itself
As in the dust it lies.

Hilda Beaumont, 1978

THE HERON AND THE GOLDFISH

A heron was strolling one day in a lake
Seeking his lunch, for his stomach did ache.
It was then that he stumbled upon a Goldfish,
And thought to himself, 'He'd look nice on a dish.'
The Goldfish looked up, but only to see
The Jaws of the Heron:
'Oh, please don't eat me!'
The Goldfish did squeal,
'Within my gold scales there are bones, not a meal!'

The Heron took in the words of the fish, and said,
'Very well, I shall grant you your wish,
But on *one* condition, that you find me my meal . . .'

The Goldfish, he darted up and about
Until he encountered a very small Trout.
He said to the Trout, 'Please come over here,'
And the Trout he did follow at the speed of top gear.
The Goldfish turned round and said to the Trout,
'I'm afraid, my dear chap, you've walked into a trap.'

'But what do you mean?'

'There's no time to explain' . . .

For the Heron's jaws were open again!

Ben Lawrence (Age 14), 1983

THE FOLLOWING DONKEY

The following, following, following Donkey
Following round the Sanctuary
Pushing his nose into people's bags
That following, following, following Donkey.

That nosy, nosy, nosy Donkey
Eating Christopher's buckle and belt
That nosy, nosy, nosy Donkey
Following people about.

That hungry, hungry, hungry Donkey
Trying to find a bit of lunch
That hungry, hungry, hungry Donkey
Trying to find a carrot to munch.

Robbie McDonald (Age 8), 1978

GOLDFISH

Goldfish, goldfish,
Swimming in your bowl
Shine shining in the sun
Like pure gold.

Goldfish, goldfish,
Swim around in circles
Now it's raining you look dull,
Not like gold anymore.

Goldfish, goldfish,
Flicker your fins
Flicker them, flicker them,
Flicker your fins.

Angela Evans (Age 8), 1980

THE ASH

The house and garden are surrounded
there are trees everywhere,
solemn pines
the sturdy firs, their branches swaying
moved by the summer breeze.
But there in the corner made by the garden wall
You stand alone.
Ash.
Not resilient as the pine,
but tall, gentle, fine and elegant
as the sun filters through your trembling leaves.
With a nature of your own
you have a gentle air, radiating tranquillity,
reflecting the peace of the summer day.
For you no squat trunk or heavy branches,
Instead,
fine strong limbs spreading gracefully into the air.
Your leaves a haze of green against the bright clear sky.
Gentle Ash
are you a happy tree,
living, growing there?
As you watch people and the seasons come and go,
secrets kept, trusts broken,
seeing all –
life, death, hate and love around you
Yet keeping all to yourself in forced silence
a silence which bears no grudge.
For you life will continue, generations will pass you by.
Unaffected by the turmoil of the world
you will live on, retaining your peace
sharing your contentment.

Susan Foster, 1973

20

MUTE TRUMPETS

They shout at me, those trumpets bright;
It seems as if their song of joy could not be missed,
The unadulterated joy of living
Which lifts the heart and catches at the throat.

Among the quilted green of yet quiescent tulips
Vast patches of a brightly tossing yellow:
A shift of scene, and there, as if by Art's design,
From a brown and broken-down old barrow
Not dead decapitated heads of daffodils,
But spilling out; cascading light;
A frozen waterfall of gold.

Alive and glowing, they prelude promises of summer,
Of light, and lazy, sunlight days.
It matters not their voice cannot be heard,
For theirs is still a shout of glory.

Yvonne Klein–Bentley, 1977

WILLOWS GROW BENT

The steely wind has turned the yellow leaves
To beggars' rags, that now lie discarded
As dying dreams upon unfeeling earth,
For squirrels to rustle among
In search of fallen acorns;
Whilst the pale sun, an old copper pendulum,
Slowly swings across the misty horizon;
And the hunched willows grow bent . . .

This is not the time to be alone.

Richard M. Gomm, 1973

THE BLOSSOM TREE IN THE GARDEN

There was a blossom tree in the garden
I remember when I was so young
It was a pretty garden but so huge,
Under the branches we swung.

I played with little Tommy Turner
We tied a swing to the tree
We danced around it like Indians
Oh what fun we had, him and me!

It had pretty pink petals
And a brown trunk so thick
And when we were tired and the sun came out
We lay on the soft green grass and slept.

And when we were asleep under the tree
A soft breeze would blow
And petals would cover us
It was like a dream.

But everything has changed now
And when I had children of my own
I used to watch them playing
But now they have gone and I'm alone.

So all I do is sit and dream
About wonderful days near the tree
And look out of the window and gaze
At the spot where the blossom used to be.

Jacqueline Longstaff (Age 12), 1978

UNDERSTANDING

It was an opportunity I could hardly refuse despite its somewhat unexpected nature; a weekend by the sea in mid March might not be everyone's ideal way of spending one's time but it had been a long, difficult term and the thought of leaving my work behind for a few days had an instant appeal. Sally and Claire had the use of a chalet in Wales for a free out-of-season holiday so immediately after lectures they loaded the car with what appeared to be enough supplies for a month and on that wet, cold, blustery Friday evening we left in search of fresh air and rest.

As the old car bumped and banged its way towards the coast, leaving in its wake the hustle and bustle of urban life, my thoughts were flowing fast and confused: work that had been completed, that which was still outstanding, relationships which had been strengthened and those which were a strain, the joys and frustrations of university life – all these crowded my thoughts making it impossible to relax.

A complete but happy silence descended upon the three of us as the Welsh mountains loomed closer. We felt more than saw their presence, for against the inky black sky they were little more than immense shadows lining our route. The wind had gradually dropped and now all was silent except for the occasional bleat of a lamb. Only a few small but welcoming lights from the windows of the isolated farmhouses scattered over the lower parts of the mountains provided an indication that we were not travelling through a dark and uninhabited country. The hypnotic motion of the car and the inspiring nature of the landscape began to have its effect upon me and gratefully I relaxed, feeling soothed by the solitude and dependency of those now towering peaks.

No one had thought to inquire about the width of the doors in the chalet, so when my wheelchair proved to be some two inches wider it presented a problem. Sally exercised her strength by

24

carrying me inside and I had to reconcile myself to remaining in one room unless necessity demanded that I move, but the contentment which had settled upon me during the journey still remained, and the pleasure which sipping hot chocolate while being warmed by the heat from the electric fire brought, dispelled any feelings of annoyance which I had experienced.

We awoke to a mild but grey and slightly damp morning, hardly surprising when one considered that it was only March. All around the chalet were signs that indeed spring was on its way and I listened with expectancy to the bleat of young lambs in the adjoining field and the 'caw-caw' of the rooks as they wheeled and circled above the bare branches of the tall oaks and elms. From the window I could see buds forming on many of the bushes in the hedgerows and in the hollow beneath a particularly weathered elm tree was a small clump of snowdrops almost hidden by the dead leaves which had drifted into the hollow during the course of the winter. With all these indications that the earth was once again coming to life, the depressing effect of the grey sky and damp atmosphere seemed unimportant as we set out in the car after breakfast. We chatted and laughed, glad to enjoy the freedom of the road and I was sincere in my mirth, yet deep within I felt the need to be silent and alone, a desire just 'to be'. Perhaps the other two sensed this need because they did not argue when I said I wanted to go off across the beach myself and after ensuring that the sand was firm enough to enable me to propel myself along and that the tide was not about to rush in and wash me over to Ireland, we bid farewell and set off in opposite directions along the wide expanse of empty beach.

For me it was a rare and beautiful experience to be alone on a beach – all too often the sand was too soft to allow a wheelchair to move across it and generally there was someone close by; a comfortable thought should I need help but also a restriction upon one's privacy. Now I could move along the water's edge and inspect the marine life which had been left exposed by the retreating tide and watch the blackheaded gulls as they skimmed across the silver-grey water or strutted confidently over the wet sand, searching with their keen eyes for any edible items. Almost imperceptibly the clouds had lifted a little, enabling a very pale yellow sun to emerge over the water. Much of the horizon and the rocks at either end of the bay were still shrouded in mist but the beach itself was bathed in a warm but pale sunlight. Conscious of the slight sucking motion of the wet sand upon the wheels of my chair, I continued towards the cliffs, stopping every once in a while to pick up those pretty shells within my reach which were partly embedded in the sand. Many were broken and smelled strongly of seaweed but I put them in my pocket nevertheless. There were two caves under the cliffs not far from the water's edge, so cautiously I made my way towards the larger of the two. Surprisingly even here the sand was firm enough to take the wheelchair. The cave went back perhaps fifteen feet and then narrowed into little more than a large crack which continued well into the heart of the cliff. I went further in, trying to avoid the icy cold water which was dripping from the arched roof. Obviously I was not the first to enter the cave, for towards the back of the cave were inscriptions on the wall left by many visitors. Some of the writing was faded and difficult to read, some fresh, probably done during last summer.

> Cath loves Jim, Pete rules O.K.
> CND 1968, June 1970

It was only then I realised I was not alone, for seated beneath and slightly to the side of these inscriptions, on a piece of rock which jutted out from the wall of the cave, was a young man. He was staring fixedly at the opposite wall and appeared to be oblivious to my presence. Grateful that I was undetected I turned to go but the sudden movement echoed in the cave and, startled, he turned towards me.

'Sorry that I startled you, I didn't notice you,' I said apologetically.

'It's quite all right,' he replied, getting up quickly as if ashamed to have been discovered. 'I was going anyway, I've been here far too long as it is.'

For the first time he appeared to realise that I was confined to a wheelchair. 'C-can I help you at all, I mean are you stuck or anything – is someone with you?' he stuttered.

'No, I shall be quite all right, my friends and I are here for the weekend and I've just come for a walk on the beach. I felt like being by myself for a while,' I explained.

He stopped as if I had said something which struck a familiar chord. 'Yes, I know what you mean. I came for some solitude myself. Suppose we all need to be alone at times although I must say it doesn't seem to help me very much at present.' He stopped abruptly as if conscious of betraying himself. Should I pursue the subject or not?

'I feel utterly content sitting here watching the waves swirling around the rocks and the gulls skimming the water. To me it's more beautiful to be here on this hazy morning than on a hot summer's day when the beach is full of holidaymakers. There's a kind of empathy with nature on days like this. So often we miss the most beautiful things. Things that are beautiful in their simplicity.'

Now it was my turn to stop, afraid that I had exposed myself to this stranger, but as I looked at him I saw that he understood and a strange look of hope appeared on his face. He crouched down until at the same height as myself.

'If only I could see things as simply as that. I'm at university and there everything is so complex and intense that you doubt the validity of everything.'

'I'm at university too; I have the same problem.'

His eyebrows lifted in surprise and I knew he was wondering how I managed, but he said nothing. 'But you said how contented you feel – how, I mean . . .' and he gestured towards the wheel-chair, indicating the frustrations I must have.

'I was tense and apprehensive last night but somehow I stopped struggling with my thoughts and saw things around me with new eyes – things coming to life, the persistent motion of the waves around these rocks, the beauty of the sunlight on the water. Nothing has changed, the work is still waiting to be completed, the difficulties which being handicapped brings are still there but right now they aren't too important, not even too real; the magnitude of all this around me puts it into perspective.'

The light had gone from his eyes; he shook his head slowly. 'I can't see things like that. I see the oil on the wings of the seagulls and the broken bottles on the beach and the hopelessness of it all. How can you, of all people, see beauty around you? I suppose you believe in God, too.'

I nodded, feeling the bitterness in his words but yet still experiencing the beauty which I saw around me. 'It just becomes more real to me with time; many people find it difficult to understand but that's the way it is,' I replied softly. He stood up and turned away, kicking roughly at the sand; the point of contact between us was lost.

Suddenly something glistened in the corner of the cave. The sunlight was falling on something making it sparkle. 'What's that in the corner?' I asked, eager to dispel the air of despondency.

'What?' he asked, turning towards me.

'There in the corner, it's glistening, near to the seaweed – surely you can see it?' I asked impatiently. 'It's really bright.' He shook his head, 'I can't see anything,' and he walked over to the corner and peered between the cracks. 'Not a thing,' he retorted.

'Well, I can see it from here, come and see.' I was determined to prove him wrong.

He came and stood at my side and shook his head, 'No, can't see anything.'

Roughly I grabbed his arm and pulled him down, forgetting he was a complete stranger.

'Now can you see it, directly in front of you!' I pointed in exasperation.

He nodded. 'Yes, there is something but you have to be low down in order to see it,' and he went over to the corner and poked about with his finger. 'Got it,' he exclaimed.

'Something valuable?' I queried.

He returned to me and placed the object in my hand. Just a piece of grey-looking stone.

'Is this all it is – but it looked . . .'

'Watch,' he said, gently taking it from me and twisting it in the rays of the sun. As the light hit the stone it gleamed and sparkled brilliantly.

'You have to look at it from the right level in the right light,' he explained.

'Yes, I know,' I replied meaningfully, looking directly at him. At last he understood.

He kept the stone and I made my way back towards the car. The mist was beginning to thicken again and soon the sun would be hidden and the greyness would return, but the sunshine, weak though it had been, and the gentle sea breeze had brought a glow to my cheeks which would not be so easily dispelled.

Hilary Stevenson, 1977

SEA TANG

From my favourite cliff-top perch, I see the sea
Stretch to the far horizon, a sparkling, twinkling blue.
Little waves creep over the wet sand, and calmly slip back,
Below me are the seagulls, soaring strong and free.

Sometimes I've seen the huge waves rise and fall,
Ridden by white sea horses, under heavy skies,
Mountainous waves, that roared and smacked and clapped,
Smashing in rage against the cracked sea wall.

On these rough days, I'd feel the gale go whistling past my ears,
And taste the keen salt tang on my cracked lips,
I'd watch the ships sail into the harbour's calmer water,
And I'd wonder at the sailors who seemed to have no fears.

From my cliff-perch I think I love it best,
At twilight, on a summer evening warm and calm,
When the sun sets in a glimmering rosy pathway on a peaceful
    sea,
The lighthouse beams, and little ships come bobbing home to
    rest.

Fay Robson (Age 12), 1981

THE DOOR

Go and open the door.
Maybe there's a mountain glittering
with snow.
Maybe there's a fair ground with
crowds of people.
Maybe there's a country side, with birds
singing and trees whispering.
Who knows what you will see.

Go and open the door.
Maybe there's a fish tank with
different coloured fish to see.
Maybe there's a wedding with beautiful
bridesmaids and a beautiful bride
Or there's a volcano with red hot flame.
Who knows what you will see.

Go and open the door.
Maybe there's a land with lots of
beautiful creatures people never knew
were alive.
Maybe there's a cave with a monster
trying to get out.
Or a sky full of stars.
Who knows what you will see.

Joanne Openshaw (Age 11), 1981

A MOMENT IN ETERNITY

Like a fractured rainbow
Flashed a kingfisher's wing
In the suspension of a moment
I heard a skylark sing
A humming bee's soft organ notes
Accompanied the song
And the Aeolian harp
Of a gentle breeze
Stirred the trees to sing along
When a Curlew joined
Its plaintive call
To the melody from the sky
The moment became adrift in time
As the memory of a sigh.

Charles Henry Stone, 1980

OF SEEING

Oh! how little I have really seen
of what is around me.
Too much I have missed.
Too much I have over-looked.
In my haste to take in
all that I could,
I have not dwelt enough
and so have failed my memory's eye.
Failing to allow each detail
to etch itself into my brain
and denying myself the chance
to later re-create, with justice,
the object of that earlier pleasure
on the canvas of my mind.
To relive that visual moment.

Overawed by the sight
of a thousand roses,
I have not seen clearly the single rose,
the simple beauty of each petal.
Warmed and comforted by a blazing fire,
I have missed the colours in its flame.
In knowing, though poorly,
the colours and forms of the landscape,
I have not noticed the fragile mosaics
created by the sky and the leaves of a birch
or the four petal perfection
and strength of pigment in a poppy.
Too casual has been my glance
and, therefore, too shallow my eye's acquaintance.
But now, with a blind man's hunger,
I must be more greedy of seeing.
Of seeing, not the whole panorama,
but the gentle detail of each optic sensation.

William Talbot, 1981

WHEN I'M AT HOME

When I'm at home I love to see the flowers in bloom and
    hops in the fields of Kent.
I love to drive over the Downs and smell the fresh-cut hay.
To see the oast houses on the farms and ships in the busy port of
    Dover.
To look over the Channel, on a clear day to see the coast of
    France.
To feel the cool wind blowing in my face and breathe the fresh
    sea air.

When I'm at school I love the smell of bacon frying in
    the pan,
The taste of Marmite spread on bread or toast.
The taste of eggs with butter, salt and pepper,
A nice white cloth with cutlery neatly spread.
To read the story of Helen Keller, Black Beauty and the tale
    of Tammy the Chimp
To read to the young ones at the weekend.
But best of all, I love to think that one day I will walk.

Linda Stevens, 1974

IMAGINATION

THE FINAL FURLONG

Jack Smithers settled into his armchair, thinking his wife Mary had done them proud with that lovely chicken dinner. It couldn't be easy for her, he mused, short of money since he'd been made redundant. His firm had closed down due to lack of orders.

The music of the television programme faded from his ears as he fell into a deep sleep. It was the voice of the racing commentator that disturbed him, with the excited tone in his voice as the horses came into the last furlong '. . . and into the last furlong they go, Blue Peter's jockey applies the whip with Happy Tizer hard on the rails but making up ground – and here comes Knobbly Knees – yes – it's Knobbly Knees first past the winning line! We'll certainly need a photograph for second and third places.' The result came up on the screen, Knobbly Knees, Happy Tizer and Blue Peter. 'So there you are,' said the commentator, 'the final few seconds of the three o'clock – Knobbly Knees the winner at twenty to one.'

Three o'clock already? Jack shot out of his chair. 'Mary? Mary?' Where's she gone? he thought. She should have woken him up ages ago.

He looked at the clock. It showed ten minutes past two. It's stopped, he thought as he took it off the wall. But no, it was still ticking. 'The hands must have stuck,' he mumbled. He waited a couple of minutes, watching the clock, but it was going all right.

His wife's wristwatch always lay in its box on the sideboard, too expensive to be worn except for special occasions. It never gained or lost a second. He picked it up and listened to the faint tick. The fingers said the time was two fifteen. Jack rubbed his eyes. Must have been dreaming, he thought.

He returned to the television screen. They were showing the horses in the parade ring for the three thirty race! He went over to the telephone and dialled the Speaking Clock.

'At the third stroke it will be two twenty precisely.'

'I'm going mad!' Jack spoke the words out loud, and again he shouted for his wife. Where on earth was she?

Again he picked up the telephone, this time dialling the number of a large bookmakers.

'Excuse me, could you tell me what won the three thirty at Nottingham?'

'What's your game, mate?' a voice replied.

'What do you mean, what's my game?'

'Look, if I could tell you the winner of the three o'clock, I wouldn't be working here as a clerk, I'd be living it up in the South of France. Your watch must be fast, mate, I should put it right. It's two twenty.' The phone was slammed down.

Jack searched around for the newspaper and looked at the line-up for the three o'clock, and sure enough, Knobbly Knees, Happy Tizer and Blue Peter were among the runners.

'It's not happening! It's just not happening!' gasped Jack. 'I'm seeing the television broadcast an hour ahead of time! I've got to do something about this! How much money have I got?' He searched in his pockets. Nothing. He rushed upstairs, lifted the carpet, then the small, loose floorboard. He took out the twenty pounds, money put there for their holiday weekend in Blackpool.

She'd go mad if he lost it, but it was like a miracle. He carefully put the folded notes into his empty wallet, raced out of the house, mounted his bicycle and rode as fast as he could to the bookmakers. He entered the office for the first time in his life. His heart was racing as he told the clerk, 'I'd like to put twenty pounds on Knobbly Knees.' The clerk asked him if it was each way or to win.

'Well – to win.'

The minutes on the bookmaker's clock seemed to drag, until finally the voice blaring out from the radio shouted, 'And they're off for the start of the three o'clock!'

Jack must have looked silly sitting there with his hands over his ears as the results came in. The man sitting next to him grinned.

'What won?' gasped Jack.

'Knobbly Knees.'

'What price?'

'Twenty to one.'

Jack felt a little unsteady on his feet as he made his way to the counter.

'There you are, the four hundred pounds,' said the clerk, handing over the money.

Jack crammed it into his saddle bag and rushed home. The television set was still on, and there on the screen were the horses lining up for the four thirty race! It was only three thirty on Jack's clock, and he sat on the edge of his seat, every muscle in his body tensed, as he watched the winner come in at thirty three to one.

Hardly able to control his shaking hands, Jack picked up the phone and dialled.

'Hello – I want a taxi to take me into town in ten minutes. Can you make it?'

'Right you are, sir.'

The taxi arrived and, clutching a brown paper bag with the money in it, Jack rushed out, forgetting to switch the television off.

But Jack was too far away to hear when the newscaster described the mugging that had taken place outside a city bookmakers where a man was killed and robbed of fourteen thousand pounds. A local man called Jack Smithers.

David J. Swift, 1981

DAVID

Green fields, spring flowers, and plateaus were my picture, as I drove through the Welsh countryside. Lambs and sheep with their bleached fleeces covered the hillside like termites on their hosts. Bluebells hung their purple heads low like guests bowing to their superior every time the wind caught them.

I didn't believe it could be so beautiful, quiet and isolated, as people had told me. So this was Wales and its hidden beauty only revealed to the visitor or traveller.

I was going to see my sister, Mary, who lived in a small village in North Wales. Being an author, working in London, Mary reckoned there would be a lot of material I could use for my books. Although I loved the countryside, I would miss the excitement of London.

I yawned and shook my head to try to keep awake. I felt tired as I had already travelled for three hours. The dusk came over the sky like a blue light cover. The sun formed a big ball of orange and red, spreading it across the sky like the smile of a child. I was moved with wonder when I saw this beautiful sunset.

I had been driving for half an hour, and I had noticed the grey dull clouds appearing in the sky. I peered out at the corner of the window and mused to myself, 'Oh no, not rain.'

The clouds formed a thick blanket of grey across the sky. Then before I knew it, gentle drops were sliding down my window-screen. Suddenly there was a flash of lightning, followed by a clap of thunder like gongs and the rain fell like buckets of water. As I saw this, my own feeling was at that moment to get out of this weather, so I put my foot hard on the accelerator.

As I came to a bend in the road, in a plateau area, I noticed a figure hovering in the darkness. As I came nearer to the spot where the figure was standing, I saw it was a young boy. I thought to myself it must be someone who had missed his bus home.

'Do you want a lift?' I shouted to the boy, opening the door of the car. He stared into the road ahead of him, but did not say anything. 'You'll get wet if you don't get in,' I shouted to him again. Still he stared into the road, not concerned by what I was saying.

'I said you'll get wet if you don't come in,' I shouted a second time. I was getting impatient.

He turned and looked at me. Seeing me, he climbed into the car.

He was a tall, slim boy, not more than twelve or thirteen years in age. He had pale skin and big brown eyes that fitted neatly into their sockets. He wore brown dirty shorts, and a shirt, with a thick green jumper over it. On his feet were a pair of white short socks and a pair of black plimsolls.

'What's your name?' I asked him, as he sat quietly in the seat. 'David,' he almost whispered, hardly moving his lips. 'That's a popular name in Wales, isn't it?' I remarked. 'Yes,' he whispered again. 'Where do you live, David?' I asked him. He didn't answer, so I guessed he was just a diffident boy.

Suddenly he touched my hand, it was icy cold, I jerked away. 'Don't go through Abergynolwyn tonight,' he said slowly. This was the village I had to drive through in order to reach my destination. 'But why?' I said, feeling a little apprehensive. 'Don't go I say,' he whispered again, his eyes blazing at me.

'Blast, I've run out of petrol,' I said worriedly, as I looked at my motor. 'That's funny, I'm almost sure before I left I filled my tank up; anyhow I've got some more petrol in the boot, wait here for me,' I said to him. I put my coat over my head and ran quickly to the boot. But to my dismay, I found nothing there. I always left some petrol in the boot for such emergencies. I blinked, and stood in the rain, as my head went blank for a minute. I felt something strange and sinister was going on, a chill ran through my body like a knife. The rain trickled down my face, like beads of sweat. I took a breath and walked back to the car.

Returning I found my quiet companion had gone. Looking up and down the road, I was unable to see anybody. Perhaps we had come to the place he lived, and he had gone off. I sighed. Turning the key to start the car, I found the usual humming sound coming out of it. I felt a huge sense of relief. There must have been a fault somewhere that had cleared itself. My watch said 7.30. I decided

41

to stay at lodgings in the village for the night, as I wouldn't make it to Merioneth tonight.

That night, I sat in the pub, surrounded by people who chatted, drank, gave big roars of laughter, and the odd person bending back on to the brown walls. The room itself was crowded and smoke from people's cigarettes, pipes and cigars formed a cloud among them.

I was talking to the landlady, who had kindly given me lodgings for the night. I asked her curiously, 'Do you know any boy by the name of David around here?' At that moment everyone stopped talking and stared at me. 'It's just that I picked him up in the rain, it was very heavy,' I quickly hastened to add. 'Where did you pick him up?' an old man asked me. He was sitting on a stool and a white mop of hair was neatly combed on his head. 'Oh, it was not far from here, about two miles from here and I remember there was a dense forest at one side as you looked through the valley,' I replied. I could feel my colour go up like mercury in a thermometer.

There was an awkward silence. The landlady offered to take me up to my room as it was getting late. I agreed to go with her.

'David was the son of that man who asked you those questions. He was a good boy, but frail. Anyway one day a circus came by, not many come here y'know. All the kids went to see it I remember, but David wasn't allowed to go. So David determined to go, went on his bike, but alas, there was a heavy storm that night, like this, and a tree fell on to poor David. He died a few days later,' the lady concluded with a sad note.

'I'm sorry,' I said.

'Don't be,' she said, then smiled and left my room.

Next morning I set off for Abergynolwyn. There was a road block there, so I slowed down my car and opened the window. The policeman told me that a landslide had occurred due to heavy rain, in this road, but had been cleared away in the early hours of the morning and was now safe to drive through. I asked him what time it had happened. 'Oh, about seven I would say,' he said, scratching his head. This was the time I had met David and he warned me not to go to Abergynolwyn. He had tried to save my life, on that same road, he tragically lost his own. Anyway I never saw David again, but I will always remember him.

Obi Chiejena (Age 15), 1981

42

RETURN JOURNEY

It was the first week in April when I decided to take a few days off from the pressures of city life, and make a return visit to my home village of Llanivery.

After three hours of high speed travelling on endless motorways, I turned off on to a minor road, which I knew would take me deep into the heart of the Welsh valleys.

This road was typically Welsh, as it casually threaded its way through lush green hills, occasionally passing an isolated farm and the ever wandering sheep.

The late afternoon mist made visibility extremely poor, the fine beads of moisture which lay gently on the windscreen were impatiently brushed aside by the wipers.

Soon my eyes became almost hypnotised by the monotonous rhythm of the windscreen wipers, my mind was being brushed back to the days of my childhood, living with my parents in the safe, cosy seclusion which was home.

Funny, even now I can actually feel the warmth and love which Mum and Dad wrapped around me; one thing is certain, no one will ever produce insulation of such quality and value.

I must have been about ten when I first realised that life could turn cold, placing sickening fear in your stomach and panic in a mind too young for rational thought.

That particular weekend Mum had been ordered to bed by the doctor. My Dad wouldn't tell me what was wrong, but as I lay in my own bedroom, I could hear Mum gasping for breath; every time I woke during the night, her breathing seemed to get faster and deeper. Oh I tried to shut out the noise by putting my head under the bedclothes, but my God, was I frightened.

After Sunday School, Dad told me, 'Go and see yer Mum then, go on, quick now mun, ask her if she'd like a drop of broth which Mrs Price just brought in.'

I dashed up the narrow staircase and into Mum's dimly lit bedroom, expecting to see her usual bright blue eyes and rosy cheeks; silly fool, that's the trouble with being young, you always have the idea that nothing changes, so for that precious split second I had completely forgotten that Mum was ill.

Instead my eyes became transfixed with shock and sorrow, as I looked at the lady, my lady, my own Mum, looking so tired and weak. She lay silently dozing, her breathing seemed easier now; maybe it was made easier by being propped up on pillows which cradled her black hair, their whiteness matching her complexion.

Her deeply sunk eyes slowly opened; she spoke softly, gulping in every ounce of air from the open door. 'Come in, bach, sit down on the bed for a moment, 'as yer Dad told you about my illness?'

I shook my head, then with one impulsive movement I buried my head in her warm breasts and began to cry. 'Hey don't cry, bach, listen to me now, Doctor Walters is sending me to hospital; don't worry bach, it's only till my old cold gets better, see.'

I didn't see; in fact the thought of my Mum going to hospital terrified me. I raised my head and looked deeply into her eyes, 'But you will be coming back, won't you, promise me Mum, please promise me.'

Her hand passed gently over my head, 'You're like yer Dad, a born worrier, 'course I'm coming back; besides, I bet you two men couldn't keep the house clean and polish the floors like I do. Now go and get some broth inside you. Oh don't matter about me, I'm not hungry, just very, very tired.'

The following morning the ambulance came, just before I went to school; the two men carried Mum on a stretcher. As she went past me in the hall, she smiled, 'Don't worry bach, I'll be back soon, promise . . .'

Just under a week later, Dad called me in from playing and told me, 'Yer Mum has gone to Jesus, lad, she won't be coming home again.' Then he turned away, pretending to look in the mirror over the mantelpiece.

I quickly grabbed at his jacket, pulling it frantically, 'But she promised Dad, she promised; besides, will Jesus love her as much as we do? Will he?' I rushed out of the room shouting as I went, 'Nobody loves my Mum as much as me, I hate Jesus, taking her away from us, I hate him.'

During the next few months, it became obvious that I'd have to go and live with my Gran, further up the valley; it was very hard for Dad trying to look after me, especially when he worked shifts down the pit.

Fair play, I enjoyed staying with Gran in her tiny cottage, with its white washed walls and slate grey floors, which she used to scrub every morning, while I prepared myself for the three mile walk to grammar school. Still, after one term me and Billy Williams found a short cut down the side of Cymla mountain and through the chapel graveyard.

Wonder what happened to Billy Williams. Oh I know only too well what happened to my dear Dad; he married again to Nancy Jones from the hardware shop.

It came as a bit of a surprise to many in the village, not least Gran and me; we only knew six months later when they came for tea and a chance to ease their conscience.

Probably Dad would have had me back home, but not her. I could see no love in her eyes for me or anyone else; she only married Dad to avoid being left on the shelf.

It was fifteen years since I had left the local grammar school to go to London and study business economics. Then I had left the village with virtually nothing; now I was returning as a business executive, with all the trappings of success, a large salary, a luxurious car and a wealth of self-confidence which often bordered on arrogance.

As I slowly drove down the winding main street of Llanivery, I realised that I'd have to stay in the one and only pub. No way could I stay with my Dad and Her; even after all this time the scars of rejection were still deep and painful.

With caution I turned into the village square; the chapel clock struck six, its mournful ring echoed through the surrounding hills, while the pale moon played hide'n'seek between the tiny cottage chimney pots.

Just opposite the chapel was the Black Horse Hotel; a rusty sign swayed gently in the evening breeze, bearing the words 'PATRONS CAR PARK AT THE REAR'.

After parking the car and collecting my weekend case, I entered the Hotel. For several minutes I stood looking at the damp-stained wallpaper, the smoke-stained ceiling and the numerous hanging cobwebs.

Eventually a large, cheerful-looking man appeared from the lounge bar; he spoke with a rich and strong Welsh voice, 'Evenin' Sir, can I 'elp you?'

I explained that I wished to spend a few days in the village. 'Can you provide me with a single room?' I asked. 'Certainly Sir, no problem, no problem at all.'

The man looked hurriedly through dust filled drawers and finally handed me a key. 'There you are, Sir; oh by the way, I'm Tom Jenkins, the landlord.'

I took the key and smiled gratefully. As I started to climb the stairs, Mr Jenkins shouted after me, 'Will you be wanting dinner, Sir?'

I thought for a moment and decided to risk it, 'Yes please, Mr Jenkins, I'll be down about eight if that's convenient.' The landlord acknowledged my statement with a broad smile.

My bedroom overlooked the main street; by the dim light of the antiquated street lamps, I could see the disused colliery and the narrow railway line, which once carried coal to Bristol. Now, the line was submerged by years of growth of grass and weeds; only two empty trucks appeared to remain intact, plus a huge pile of small coal.

After dinner, which had been adequate but not outstanding, I moved into the lounge bar; a thick curtain of cigarette and pipe smoke filled the room, and it was obvious from the babble of Welsh, that most of the clientele were locals.

Mr Jenkins leaned on the bar counter. 'Enjoy your meal, Sir, fair play, my Mrs is a good cook, isn't she?' I agreed without showing too much enthusiasm, sat on a bar stool and ordered a large scotch.

Passing my drink, Mr Jenkins looked at me with interest and cautiously asked, 'Are you from round 'ere? My reason for asking is because a while back Will Jones' boy went to some college or other in London. I don't know what became of 'im, but you look exactly like 'im.'

'Will Jones was my father, he worked at the colliery for over thirty years. However, I wanted something more from life; now I'm a business executive with a London finance company.'

Standing with hands on hips, Mr Jenkins exclaimed, 'Dew, dew, looks as if you've done all right for yourself, fancy suit, big car, yes, you've done all right.' Mr Jenkins continued, 'Do you remember the previous landlord, Tudor Evans? He died in a car accident further down the valley, oh must be about six years ago. Some folks round 'ere say he haunts the village; mind you, I takes no notice, well, not normal is that.'

The atmosphere of the Black Horse was typical of a local pub, village gossip mixed freely with laughter, discussions led to arguments and so on. In between pulling pints of Welsh bitter, I asked Mr Jenkins how long the colliery had been closed.

He scratched his thinning, grey hair and looked thoughtfully towards the ceiling. 'Must 'ave been about '65 when the NCB decided to shut the colliery, 'asty decision mind; one mornin' an official came down and told the workers that it was no longer a profitable pit. As you can see they left nearly twenty ton of good quality coal behind. Such a waste, no one will bother to move that lot now, see, such a waste.'

As I sat slowly sipping my final whisky, I gazed into the last glowing embers of the log fire; a feeling of warm contentment swept over me, so I retired to my bedroom for a good night's sleep.

My room was situated in the attic of the Hotel; the damp walls and sloping ceiling gave the room a very claustrophobic effect. The chapel's clock tower cast a deep shadow across the room; compared with the hustle and bustle of the bar, this room had a ghostly silence. Still, it took me only minutes to undress and wrap myself between the crisp, white sheets.

While lying there naked and waiting for sleep to arrive, I smiled and thought, if Gran could see me now; she always insisted that I should wear proper warm woolly vests and pants under thick striped pyjamas.

This rule applied even in summer. I often grumbled 'I'm awful hot Gran, can I leave my 'jamas off?' but there was little point in asking.

Gran would stand over the bed waving a menacing finger at me, 'Now listen 'ere bach, while you are in my 'ouse, you'll dress decent like. Besides the Lord looks down on you every night; if you're not dressed proper, well, the Devil himself will put evil thoughts in your 'ead.'

Considering this attitude exists even now in Wales, it was a wise move on my behalf not to bring Angela with me. No doubt

Mr Jenkins would have known we are not married, therefore we would have spent a chilly night in the car park.

One of the less essential assets of the Welsh is that they can smell immorality with the same degree of efficiency as a police dog sniffs out drugs.

Casually I passed my hand over the empty half of the bed, thinking of Angela and how she and London life had broadened my mind in the most delightful manner.

Slowly my eyes began to feel heavy, the small bulb in the faded lampshade became a blur, I fell asleep to the sound of the gentle wind which whistled through the rotting window frame.

My deep slumber was initially disturbed by the sound of men's voices, not exactly shouting, more like giving instructions. I lay still for a while trying to gather my thoughts.

Then I heard the clanking of coal trucks being shunted together by a hissing steam engine; by this time I was wide awake and decided to get up and investigate.

The night air was bitterly cold on my naked body and I began to shiver violently. I slowly made my way to the narrow window. Looking out on to the dimly lit street, I could see a group of ten or twelve men digging feverishly at the huge pile of coal.

Both coal trucks were being filled rapidly by the men, while the small steam engine patiently waited. Once the trucks were full the engine chugged off into the darkness; minutes later it returned and the loading process began once more.

After observing this action for some while, my curiosity became overwhelming. I hurriedly dressed, ran down the two flights of the Hotel stairs and out into the main street.

I ran frantically towards the colliery, gulping in the freezing night air as I went. On reaching the tall gates of the colliery, I stumbled to the ground with exhaustion. Slowly rising to my feet I looked around, but to my complete amazement the site was entirely deserted.

My hands, numb with cold, clung tightly to the rusted, iron gates, my eyes searching the darkness for any signs of activity, but soon my vision became blurred and I remember little else.

The next time my eyes opened, I found myself in bed but fully clothed. The morning sun squeezed its way through the faded bedroom curtains and the chapel bell struck eight, so I swiftly washed, shaved and went down to breakfast.

During breakfast I related the whole night's proceedings to the landlord. Finally I asked, 'Well, what do you make of it, Mr Jenkins?'

The man looked doubtfully at me for a few moments and frowned deeply. 'Sorry bach, I just don't understand your story, in fact I don't even know why you be calling me Mr Jenkins.'

I looked up in utter confusion as the landlord continued, 'I'm Tudor Evans and I've been the landlord 'ere for the past six years.' Slowly my head sank on to my chest and my hands started perspiring freely.

As if in a hypnotic trance, I dashed back upstairs and began packing. My mind was completely closed to any logical thoughts or reasonable explanations; I was behaving like a child in insecure surroundings.

Minutes later, I was standing by the deserted bar, shouting for some attention, 'Mr Jenkins, no sorry, Mr Evans, anyone here, anyone here?'

The front door opened and the landlord staggered in with a large cardboard box. 'Sorry if I've kept you waitin' Sir, but I 'ad to collect the groceries for the Mrs.'

He placed the box on the edge of the bar, then glanced down at my case. 'You're not leavin' already are you, Sir? Pity, it looks like bein' a nice spring day. Honest now, as I came up the road, the sun was makin' the daffs shine like gold, beautiful it was, really beautiful.'

Frantically my brain raced to find a suitable reason for my sudden departure, but I resorted to a sentence which any fool would see through, 'I'm sorry but I must return to London, it's a meeting, yes, that's it, a meeting which I had forgotten about.'

The landlord made out a bill and handed it to me, then he looked long and hard. 'Do you know Sir, I've a feelin' you'll be returning one day.'

Owen Davies, 1983

THE ELEVEN
THIRTY-THREE

The biting north-easterly wind swept driving snow across the deserted platform of the small Yorkshire station. The old gaslamp mantles flickered as strong gusts of wind caught their flames casting strange shapes and long shadows into the many nooks and crannies of the solid stone building. Inside the warm booking office old Sam Arkwright sat in front of a glowing fire gently dozing to the rhythmic tick-tock of the large clock that hung over the window. The sound of a distant klaxon horn aroused the porter; he craned his scrawny neck and after a few seconds focused his eyes on the Roman numerals – 11.15 p.m. 'Good,' he thought, 'another six or seven minutes and the last train from the Junction will be in, then off home to bring in the New Year with the wife.'

Sam stretched himself and looked around the small, snug office with its mahogany counter and ticket cabinet. Everything appeared to be in order. The old oil handlamp was at the ready beside the antiquated ticket date-stamping machine which he had changed some hours earlier. This practice of changing such machines before the last departure was strictly against Company rules, but old Sam knew from years of experience, forty-seven to be exact, that there would be no passengers for the last train. The wooden chair creaked as he arose. He shuffled across to the brown, cracked and chipped sink in the corner, half filled a dirty milk bottle with cold water and returned to the fireplace and doused the glowing embers. The shutter across the ticket window rattled. 'Wind must be getting up,' he thought, and proceeded with his chores. The shutter rattled again. This time it was a definite rat-ta-ta-tat. He arose from his knees and walked across to the window and undid the brass snecks and raised the well-worn heavy shutter. Through the glass partition he could see a khaki greatcoat with gleaming brass buttons. He was unable to see a face.

'Aye lad, can I help thee?' he asked in his warm Yorkshire accent.

'Is the eleven thirty-three running on time?' a deep voice boomed.

The old porter gave a look of amazement. 'Ee lad, the eleven thirty-three hasna' run these last twenty-five years.'

'But we were told that it caught the Midnight south.'

'An' so eet did lad, but that hasna' run for the same twenty-five year,' Sam told him, beginning to lost patience.

'How then do we get to transit camp?' the voice asked.

'Walk,' Sam suggested, slamming the shutter down.

There was a great deal of noise coming from the platform as he returned to the grate: the noise continued and after a few minutes the old man decided he had better investigate the commotion. After all, he was in charge and if anything went wrong on Company property he was responsible. He picked up the hand-lamp and went out on to the platform. The snow had stopped falling and in the moon and gaslight he saw several men in the King's uniform. Several were milling about the platform while others were huddled in small knots talking amongst themselves. Great gales of laughter were coming from the group furthest from the office door. Sam recognised the loud laughter – it was his brother David's. He began to walk towards the group that the hilarity was coming from. Just before he drew level with them he heard a sound that he had not heard in well over ten years – that of a steam engine.

'Impossible,' he thought, turning around. Sure enough an old tank engine pulling three coaches was clearly outlined against the snow-covered embankment. The train steamed slowly and noisi-ly into the tiny wayside station. There was something strange about the old-fashioned train – it was in total darkness.

Suddenly doors were flung open and shafts of yellow light shone on the white platform and the now freezing snow glistened as the light struck it. Doors banged shut and Sam heard a voice shout, 'Never mind lads, this time next week we'll all be sunning in Africa.' Gales of laughter followed the comment.

The guard's whistle shrilled through the clear night air and the driver pulled on the engine whistle cord. The engine hissed and threw bright red sparks into the deep velvet night sky. Steel screeched against steel as wheels slipped against rails struggling for friction, steam hissed and the ugly engine belched clouds of black smoke heavenwards. Slowly the black shadow began to move and in a few seconds had pulled away from the platform leaving only the regular clickety-click of wheels going over rail joints ringing in Sam's ears. The old man looked up the line towards the Junction but no red tail-lamp could be seen.

Terrified the old porter walked back to the warmth of the booking office. He was trembling as he closed the door and looked up at the clock, 11.34 p.m. Sam pulled himself together and continued with his chores. He was glad when a few minutes later he heard the familiar klaxon as the two-coach multiple diesel unit pulled into the station. He went out to the platform and positioned himself at the exit. The brightly lit train drew to a stop in front of him and Major Burton Brigg alighted. As the Major walked towards him Sam heard the guard give two distinct buzzes and the diesel revved and swiftly moved off. The man gave him a wave as the open door drew level with the exit and then slammed it shut.

'Evening Major,' Sam said as he took the tall upright man's ticket. 'Late tonight.'

'Yes, Sam. Funny thing that – um – could have sworn I heard a steam train just this side of the Junction. Funny – um – just like the wartime blackout, heard it but never saw it. Very peculiar,' the Major told him in a clipped voice.

'Funny indeed, sir,' Sam agreed, and was about to relate the strange events of a few minutes earlier when the Major spoke again.

'Well, can't stand here talking all night.' He moved off down the station driveway. 'A happy New Year to you Sam,' he shouted. 'And the same to you, sir,' Sam replied and turned and walked along the platform.

He pulled the chains of the gaslamps as he went, putting their flickering flames out. He looked at the deserted snow-covered platform. It was covered with dozens of footprints. He shuddered and returned to the booking office. Inside he had a last look around – everything was in order. He switched off the bare light, locked the office door securely and walked smartly to the station gate and swung the heavy ornate ironwork closed and padlocked it. He walked down the snow-covered driveway to the main road. There was only one set of footprints on the driveway, those of the Major. He almost ran to the main thoroughfare. There was no traffic moving as he walked towards the village. A million stars twinkled above him as he made his way towards his cottage and warmth. The clock in the tower of the Norman church in the centre of the village was striking midnight as he passed. 1978 had arrived. The singing of 'Auld Lang Syne' could be heard coming from The Lamb's Head. Sam paused and looked across to the simple war memorial on the edge of the green. He crossed and read the inscription:

TO THE MEMORY OF THE SON OF THIS VILLAGE
1939–1945
David Arkwright   Aged 18
Lost at Sea 1st January, 1942
His name liveth forever

Archie C. Savage, 1978

A FLY'S EYE VIEW

I would just like to introduce myself. I am George and I am a fly. I love to fly around old buildings and new ones where people are living because there is a lot to explore. I start off in the kitchen and work my way round the house. But let's just concentrate on the kitchen for a moment. I would just like to describe a plate to you in my own way.

To a fly a plate is really giant in size but fun to run round getting dizzy all the time and not knowing when to get off. Now on to the table which takes a lot of time to explore. It is very large you see and I am very small. I am now going on to the cup. When I see a cup of tea I climb up and look in, then suddenly I go cross-eyed at what I have just seen. My life seemed to flash in front of me. I could have fallen in and drowned or been burnt to death. If you saw me there you would try to swipe me unaware. I take it you think I am very dirty. Well that might be true but I have got to have my fun just the same as you. I like you, why can't you like me? If you read the rest of the story it may help you see just how much in common other things have with me. I may be a bit of a nuisance but people are not so great themselves.

To some people I am just a bionic dirtspot that doesn't do anything but get in the way; that seems to be the reason you squash my mates to death with a paper. Have you ever thought I could have been brought into the world for the same purpose as you? I might sit on the table and crawl all over the bread but surely that is better than the things some of you humans do like sticking a knife into each other, so why not spare a thought for us? After all, you only live once. Think of all the things you can do to us and the little we do to you. If you didn't leave your bread and other foodstuffs out flies like myself would not be tempted to come into your house and fly about and annoy you. So if you think about it it is really your own fault. I am not really in the position to tell you what to do but the state the world is in today we could do without a war between humans and flies, don't you think?

Dogs and cats are just as bad as flies at times. Especially if you have got a family to look after because you have to make sure your husband and children get all the attention they need and then you have to make sure the dog gets just as much attention as the husband and children. You also have to train the dog and take it out for walks and pay to get food for it as well as your own. This all costs a lot of money and you have to watch that you can afford to keep it. You then have to make sure it doesn't go into other people's gardens and do the toilet against the wheel of someone's car or against a lamp-post as some people will object to this and are quite right too. Dogs can be more dirty than we are and more bother too. So let me ask you, why oh why can't you leave us alone to live in peace?

Now that I have asked you to let my friends be I would just like to tell you what some other things are like to me. Let's take a sewing machine. It is very good to explore because I can see the different patterns the thread makes and I can watch the needle going up and down as the material moves along and if it is worked by a foot pedal I can sit on the floor and watch it going up and down and if it is worked by a wheel I can sit on it and go round and round. Oh it can be fun but then again it can also be dangerous too. If I happened to slip and get caught under that sharp needle I would be a goner so I have got to be very careful. A fly's life can be very short – here today and gone tomorrow.

Another place I like to explore is the kitchen but I have got to be very careful in there as there are all sorts of sharp things lying around. One thing I have never gone near is the oven as I have always had visions of me getting inside and the door closing behind me. We are always risking our lives to explore things but not the oven. At least not for me.

Just as you have your population problems we have ours. It seems to be increasing every year. But at least we can spread ours out as we can just fly off to other countries without any red tape. Not like the trouble you go through to get anywhere. When we are great in numbers we feel stronger as some women are more afraid of us than we are of them. And when you think about it it is really silly. Look at the size of us compared with them. There is no way we could ever do anything to hurt them but they can easily knock us on our back. It is really funny. Oh, by the way, in case you have been misled, I am black not blue. There are many strange things you humans do that we don't understand like this particular thing. When you are sitting for quite a long time and breathing in the same air for a while you make a noise like this, *atishoo atishoo*, and then you get a small piece of cloth out and wipe your nose. This to us is very strange but flies have a lot to learn.

I like to go to school to see the children at work but I do not like the sound of teachers when they shout and bang the desk with a ruler. I like to paint but I don't like getting my feet all paint. You see I have to stand on the paper while I am doing the picture. When the school bell rings I nearly jump three feet in the air. This is where I have to be careful again because I don't want someone's big feet on top of me. I come across quite a lot of feet when I am at school so by the time I have jumped out of the way of all of them I am quite dizzy.

I also like to visit hospitals but I don't get there too often. Why? Because they keep their wards so clean and sterile I don't like to dirty them. But I remember one visit all I could see was humans lying on beds. Some looking as if they will never make it, others looking not too bad. Then I went to the operating room and saw some of you being cut up, but when I saw you later you looked O.K. so I can't say I understand why they cut you up in the first place. I never land in the part where all the knives and sharp jaggy things are; if they can cut you up think what they can do to me. Not only that, I am a coward – I hate to admit it but I am scared stiff at the sight of blood.

Another exciting but dangerous place is a disco. I went to one once and when I was walking along the floor all of a sudden – splash – I got soaked with some Coca-Cola and then I nearly got suffocated by a crisp poke. I decided to fly to one of the tables but I misjudged and ended up in a jug of orange juice. All of a sudden I remembered I couldn't swim and I didn't have my armbands. But I was lucky because someone came for a drink and spilt the juice all over the table and I managed to scramble out of the puddle. After that I decided I had had enough for one day. So I went off for a nice long sleep. When I met my friends the next day they asked me where I was and what had happened so I told them I had had a date. And they believed me.

I hope what I have told you helps you understand my life. So I hope now you will think before you kill myself or any of my friends. But if you still declare war we flies can be as vicious as you when it comes to it. I don't like threatening you but I feel as though I am not getting through. We would like to be your friends but you don't seem to do anything about it like working something out between us. I keep mentioning it but it is because I really would like to be your friend and I wish you would like to be mine. I wish I could speak to you personally but as I can't this is the next best thing.

I am going to tell you about how we older flies look after the younger ones. We sleep on bits of bread or cheese. We don't sleep on the cheese very much if we can help it as its smell is overpowering at times. We show them how to climb into bins to get food and then we make them take some exercise and this is when they tend to explore and end up annoying you. But they are only young and don't realise they are doing anything wrong, but they will soon learn.

I think that about sums up our lifestyle. I hope you found it interesting, as I enjoyed writing it. Apart from just enjoying it I hope you learned something from it and I will be looking forward to seeing you around.

Have a happy Easter and don't leave your Easter eggs out where my friends and myself can get at it and if you do don't say I didn't warn you . . .

Yvonne Burns (Age 15), 1977

THE PAPER WAR

The future looks very bleak, not just for me, but for the whole of our army. Our Queen was captured a few weeks ago, and since then we have just gone to pieces, for it was she who kept us together. Poor thing, she must be having a terrible time at the moment with those barbarians, or Africans as they like to be called. They are savages, they really are. They chased our poor Knights all around the battlefield. When they had them trapped, they just carried on chasing them, and did not dispose of them until they gained position and weakened our defence.

Before I go any further telling you about all the people that have been captured, I had better explain what this is all about. You see, the Blacks declared war on us, the British (or the Whites as we are nicknamed), six weeks ago. The reason for this was that about a year ago we refused to export paper to them. They said they wanted a good explanation why we exported paper to Japan and America, but not to them. We told them that we did not have enough to export to all three countries, and as they did not trade as much with us, we would leave them out. But, of course, that silly Queen of theirs said that her husband, the King, did everything he possibly could for us, especially when we were in trouble. (This is a load of rubbish, because all they did was send us a simple plan of a castle, which was no good to us at all.) We explained as nicely as we could that the next lot of paper that came out of the mill, surplus to our requirements, would go straight to them. This is the reason they declared war.

Unfortunately, they have the strongest position at the moment, and have had for the last week or two. The size of the two armies was equal, but now they have about seven hundred more men than us.

I heard, from a reliable source, that our King has devised a plan, but, however, if he is able to put this plan into practice, he might have to sacrifice a few soldiers. And I might be one! What he intends to do is to move a couple of ranks of soldiers down to their territory and to attack the Bishops, because at the moment they are holding a useful position in their defence. This attack, we hope, will weaken their defence and leave a gap so we can get to their castles. We can't attack for a few days yet, because the King is in a very tricky position, and has been since the Queen's capture, may I add.

The King has appointed himself to look after all the nearby land and stop any risings while we attack the Bishops. He had warned us that while we attack we must be on the lookout and report anything that is suspicious or any moves that do not have reason.

We got orders to attack a week later – all seemed to be going fine, too fine for my liking, for they let us capture their Bishop. We told the King that we thought this was rather odd, because usually, well, let's say in the past, they have not surrendered quite so easily. But he said they were probably tired, and getting fed up, so told us to carry on with the plan.

A few days after getting the order to carry on, we were told to try desperately to get to the base of their territory and recover our Queen, because the King's position had worsened; he said he thought it might be over within the next few days. After hearing this, we knew the position must be bad for in the past he had always been optimistic. We tried our hardest, and I mean our hardest, to get to the base, but it was too well protected. We even tried the old trick of losing men to make a hole in their security, but that did not work.

'Checkmate. I told you I'd beat you didn't I, but you said that no one could beat the brilliant British at chess. Well, you're wrong aren't you? And before you leave the lab, I'll have the typing paper,' said Tom.

'All right, all right, you win, but the next time I'll get you in the four-move-mate,' I said.

'I don't care, just get the typing paper, I've got history next lesson.'

'Here's your typing paper.'

Ruth Bailey (Age 13), 1976

THE SILENT ONES

From time to time there's been a fuss
About the Hippopotamus,
Or, perhaps, some garbled rumour
Of a ghost-like, roaming Puma;
But now, I'm minded to declare
My knowledge of some beasts quite rare.
Although you'll think it most absurd,
They're kinds of which *you've* never heard!

There is the grotesque Rumblecrunch
Which chews glass bottles for its lunch
And up-ends all the litter-bins
In search of tasty cocoa-tins,
Or gobbles (with delighted hic's)
Hundreds of thrown down lollie-sticks;
And when it needs to slake its thirst
It shuffles round, with lips all pursed
Waiting to play its usual prank
Of sucking petrol from a tank;
A pastime where it has the pull
Because it's quite *invisible*.
Glum policemen all frustrated,
By their Sergeant castigated,
Are doomed to hold a hopeless brief
In vain attempts to catch a thief.
Then there's the wily Tellyblog
Who make the screen look wreathed in fog,
With wavy lines and flashing blobs;
In vain you twiddle all the knobs!
And now and then, just for a lark,
He makes the picture go quite dark!
His cousin, the Electroleen,

Stops traffic lights from turning green;
With mocking laughter hoots and howls
To see car-drivers' savage scowls.
He's the young friend we should accuse
When we our wits and tempers lose
And say: '*Another* fuse that's blown!'
It's *him* of course, had we but known.

★ ★ ★

Maybe I'd better call a halt and not say any more
In case a tiny pavement mole is lurking near my door;
He'll root beneath the paving-stones and cause the earth to slip,
Which makes the rim rise up a bit, and over it I'll trip;
Or else, when it's been raining and my roadside walk I take,
All unaware, I'll step down SPLOSH! into a mini-lake!
So this is all I have to say about that silent throng
Because they've quite a genius for making things go wrong.
It's not *all* due to carelessness; my foolish need for haste
Which makes me rip my typing up; much time and paper waste!
I'm well aware the facts, as shown, can't be sustained by proof
But if you weigh them carefully, there *might* just be *some* truth;
One *does* find broken glass around and upturned litter-bins
And thrown down lollie-sticks abound, and so do cocoa-tins;
Who *hasn't* had some trouble with their television screen?
And now and then a traffic light *won't* change from red to green;
Who *hasn't* tripped up paving-stones or called themselves a fool
For stepping, willy-nilly, in an unsuspected pool?
I've given *you* the warning; *Your* choice to scoff or heed,
But watch out for THE SILENT ONES that do the dirty deed!

Thomas W. Berris, 1977

THE CHILDREN NEVER THOUGHT OF NOT GOING

On Saturday morning Mike woke up fairly early. The sun was shining as though it was a summer morning but it was autumn. Mike looked out of the window to see whether it was windy enough to fly his kite. It wasn't raining as it had been for the last few days. Looking out he saw this massive great hole right in the middle of the garden. Mike couldn't believe his eyes. 'Good gracious, that wasn't there yesterday,' Mike yelled to his sister Sandra. 'You'll never guess what's in the garden,' gasped Sandra in astonishment. 'Well, let's go and explore it,' shouted Mike. They charged downstairs (didn't bother to have breakfast of course) and pulled on their coats from the hook in the hall and ran outside. They raced to the hole. Mike won. The hole was deep! You could have dropped the garden shed in it twice over. They had to get a ladder to get down – it never occurred to them not to go down. The sides were slimy and the ladder slipped a bit, but they managed. At the bottom they saw a narrow tunnel just high enough for them to stand in. The sides were slimy too. The children crept down the tunnel. It was not quite dark and Mike and Sandra were rather frightened. They didn't know what they would come across down in a strange dark tunnel. A sharp turn and the tunnel became quite light and . . . they could hear curious sounds in the distance. Sandra was getting very frightened. 'Can we go back now Mike? I'm frightened,' she said nervously. 'No, not now we've got this far,' said Mike, trying to figure out what the light and noise was. 'Oh, all right,' said Sandra, not very cheerfully.

They had to walk on quite a bit further. Then, they both gasped with amazement. Neither of them made a sound until Mike gulped, 'It looks as though some giant worms or some kind of creatures are having a tea party,' he whispered. 'I don't like it. I'm going back right this minute,' Sandra whispered anxiously. She started to walk back but Mike took hold of her arm. 'Look, Sandra, just stay with me and you won't get hurt. Anyway they look very friendly.' 'I hope I can trust you, Mike.'

After Mike and Sandra had plucked up courage they walked nearer to the table where the creatures were sitting. Now they could see that they were giant worms. They all had party hats on and brightly coloured ties. One worm in a white and blue tie with a white hat said, 'Come and join us.' 'Would you like a sandwich?' another worm asked politely. Another said, 'Have a seat, you two.' Mike and Sandra were very nervous of joining a party with giant worms. The chairs were very large. The children had a job to climb up them. As it was their chins were nearly touching the large table. The plates were the size of a dustbin lid. The sandwiches were ten times bigger than ours. Mike and Sandra shared half a sandwich between them; it was ample. 'What are your names?' said a worm wearing a brown and orange tie. Mike answered, 'My name is Mike, this is my sister Sandra.' 'Where do you come from?' 'We come from Tolworth,' said Sandra who had calmed down now that she realised that the worms were friendly. Mike and Sandra had forgotten all about breakfast and getting back home again. Suddenly Sandra screamed. She could see about five snakes all blocking the gangway of the tunnel. These snakes were not at all friendly, they were enemies to the worms. The snakes had a deal with the worms that they would have a war because the snakes wanted a tunnel where the worms lived. It wasn't really fair but the worms were too frightened to argue. 'Oh, no,' the chief of worms said, 'I forgot it was war today, I thought it was next week.' 'Nooooo.' The chief of snakes' voice was very deep so it echoed right through the tunnel. 'We had a deal and you cannot break it,' the large snake said. 'Oh, all right,' said the chief of worms. The chief of worms didn't want to fight because the snakes were much stronger than the worms and he knew he would lose, but they could have a chance because there were more worms than there were snakes. At last they were ready to start the battle. The worms charged towards the snakes and surprisingly the snakes crawled backwards. Mike and Sandra were surprised and all the worms were surprised. The snakes kept on going backwards because the worms' shields were extremely shiny and the snakes could see themselves in them and were terrified. In the end the snakes turned round and started to run; they kept on running until they reached their home. 'I never thought they were such chickens,' said the chief of worms. 'They will never come back again,' said Mike. After a while the chief of worms said, 'We'd better get to bed now, would you two like to stay with us?' 'Thank you but we'd better be getting back now,' said Sandra. So Sandra and Mike waved goodbye and they ran back through the tunnel and climbed up the ladder and went indoors. 'Breakfast is nearly ready children so go and wash your hands,' said the children's mother when they had just come through the door. 'What's the time,' asked Sandra. 'Only eight,' said their mother. 'But we've been in the garden all day,' said Sandra. 'No, we have only just got up,' said their mother. After breakfast Mike and Sandra went upstairs to get their kites; they looked out of the window expecting the hole to be there but to their surprise it wasn't.

'Was it a dream or not?'

Sarah Rees (Age 11), 1980

CAT ON COOL TILES

The injured Siamese cat sat still and silent upon the cool, glistening tiles of the mantelpiece. It radiated a kind of detached dignity, which might have been that of a frozen but determined Christian martyr. The guilty boy, joyless and appalled, stared up at his victim, with something of the horror of a convicted sinner overtaken by events before the judgment throne.

There were in the sitting-room, however, no voices of angels or celestial choristers – only the twittering of sparrows beyond the open window and the whispering of respectful leaves, awed by the passing of the summer breeze.

A sense of eternity there certainly was – in the unvarying, rhythmic and terrifyingly slow ticking of the old Tompion clock, whose hands pointed appropriately straight up to heaven! There was eternity, too, in the utter immobility of everything in the room. It was as if one of the old Dutch masters had caught them all transfixed in one of his spell-bound interiors. The cat did not spring; the clock did not strike; the boy did not stir. He stood like a statue on the white sheepskin mat. For a moment, the twentieth century was remote and irrelevant – save that a little green leaf, egged on by the breeze, slipped in at the window, spiralled down to the carpet, and lay fittingly inert in front of the empty hearth.

There *was* movement, however, although hidden and suppressed. The cat and the clock, had they been able to speak, could have spoken of the scarcely visible rising and subsiding of Hereward's suddenly tightening breast. His young heart seemed to be bumping and jumping about, hurling itself against his ribs, and getting in the way of his breath. They could have spoken, too, of the anguished, desperate working of his eyes as he raised mute appeals for help to the ceiling and beyond. He had a sickening apprehension that, if his mother should happen to enter just then, heaven might decline to involve itself in his affairs, especially in view of the enormity of his offence. He had done the deed. Between him and Chang there was now a great unbridgeable gulf fixed, far wider and more daunting than the physical distance between the carpet and the cat.

Hereward was eight, and strong in both body and character. Had he been weaker in body, he might not have hurt Chang, but a small boy cannot be blamed for being well-built, muscular and active, nor for wanting to experiment and investigate. It was not that he hated Chang, either. Nor did he wish to be cruel. For all his red hair, broad back and sturdy thighs, he was really a very sensitive child. When his eyes flashed, it was not usually with aggression but more often out of a sense of righteous indignation over the treatment and troubles of some less fortunate or less stalwart creature. Just now, however, there was no sparkle in the eyes. He was himself the little one in distress, and, to make it worse, his distress arose from having harmed a dumb thing beloved of his darling mother.

Chang was a blue-point Siamese of the most aristocratic type. Hereward's mother had told him enchanting stories of the Kings of Siam, a name which conjured up far more romantic pictures than its ugly modern title ever could. He had often dreamed himself across the seas and into the palaces of the wealthy owners of such majestic cats, imagining himself a prince surrounded by feline beauty. Whenever he looked at Chang he was overcome with admiration for the cat's smooth symmetry and delicate colouring. The eyes were blue, and they glistened and sparkled magically. One could fancy that Merlin had transformed himself into this shapely creature, and was looking out upon the world with a view to performing some mighty feat of magic, or of mesmerising some hapless tiny mouse into putting a foot fatally too far forward. They were slant eyes, giving the cat an inscrutable appearance very suitable for one originating from a land so close to China. He loved the combination of mystery and majesty, streamlining and sleekness.

Chang was usually to be found on the top of the mantelpiece. His blueness stood out dramatically against the cream of the tiles which were his throne. One could pick out the tiniest details of each paw and claw, the intricate patterns of dark and light in the finely blended coat, and the grace and tightness of each curve and fold of that sinuous figure. Hereward's mother sometimes

66

allowed Chang to sit in the hearth, staring into the fire, but the boy preferred to see him on the mantelpiece so that he was 'high and lifted up' like the Great One in the Bible.

Now, as a sad and fearful eternity held them all in a motionless silence the maltreated cat seemed to be considering some calculated course of action. Its eyes glittered with a certain intense malignity Hereward had never experienced before. They seemed to be saying, 'It will be your turn next, hateful boy, so just you wait!' Hereward felt a sort of wave-like, shifting movement underneath his ribs, as if some essential part of his body had become separated from its neighbours. Chang, like many orientals, had the uncanny knack of apparently being able to look in two directions at one and the same time. Now Hereward felt the full glare of one blue eye boring into his soul while the other appeared to be gazing intently at the heedless sparrows on the crazy paving, outside the window. It was an unnerving sensation, tending to turn one's once strong, healthy legs into useless unsupported pieces of rubber tubing!

Still rigid, still outwardly frozen like a statue, he allowed his even gaze to rest upon the poor creature's tail. In the first shock of his remorse, he had not dared even to glance at it. The whole thing had been a ghastly act of unsuspected stupidity. Now it was too late. He had rushed in from a wild game of cowboys and indians with some unruly friends and, seeing Chang sitting on the favourite part of the mantelpiece, had whooped at him brandishing his tomahawk and shouted.

'Talk! Confess, or I strike!' The cat had naturally not known what to say and, without giving it even a moment for reflection, Hereward had indeed struck very viciously and with that terrifying, subconscious savagery, which is not too far below the surface of our scarcely skin-deep humanity. The blow had been struck, and now the horrified boy studied the place where blood must inevitably gush forth.

The eternity of the soul cannot prevent the orderly succession of more mundane affairs. The soft summer breeze nudged aside the branches of the silver birches outside the window, and the sun slipped into the sitting-room. Without any obvious movement it bathed the walls and furniture in a peaceful golden glow. Some of it fell upon Chang's head and shoulders, turning him into a sphinx, and the tiles of the fireplace into a shimmering desert. The irises and pupils of the cat's eyes became those of a lion about to spring and claw and rend. They were grey with rage and pent-up revenge. The little boy, almost stifled now with terror, felt once again the disintegrating sensation within his breast, a sort of going-away of things that should be fixed, together with a shocking release of water between his legs.

It was midday and he was in his own sitting-room but he seemed to be in a timeless, unknown and paralysing world in which everything happened *to* one and nothing could be done *by* one. He knew that he should have rushed to the toilet or squeezed his legs together, or run for his mother, or shouted, or done *something* – but he remained petrified and eviscerated and foul. It was midday, but he had become part of a nightmare. He *hoped* it was a nightmare.

The sun was flooding the room with a dazzling brightness. Now he knew what was happening. God had come in. God had seen what Hereward had done, and had come to deal with him. Now it would be useless to try to run to or call his mother. She had herself often informed him reassuringly that God was greater than anyone else, only this time it was in no way reassuring. What use was his mother now? One was alone with one's tomahawk, the mortally injured cat, and the puddle at one's feet. For the first time in his short existence, Hereward became aware that there were situations and emotions which appeared to have no solution, and which could not be controlled.

The sun was not only dazzling. It was also very hot, and he remembered that hell was hot. He stood transfixed with inexpressible terror as if cemented to the floor. He knew that he could not summon enough strength to raise one foot from the carpet, yet God was about to carry him off in a twinkling. He knew that there could only be unending suffering for those who did not repent. Yet he could not get his mouth to open and blurt out the necessary words, 'I'm sorry – I will never do it again!' It was bewildering that, while the lower part of his body allowed things to escape, the other part was all shut up and dry. It was awful and inexplicable that Chang continued to look in two directions and that one of those directions was straight at him, the boy with the tomahawk, the boy who had struck, the boy who had . . .

A sparrow, quite unaware of the tragic events that were taking place in the sitting-room, hopped intrusively on to the windowsill. He pecked about for a moment or two, and then leaned his head on one side, and surveyed the interior. His mate flew down beside him. Wings and feathers fluttered and then they both darted off into the branches of the trees. That had been quite an adventure – encountering *the boy* in his den – but they had survived and could tell the tale to a large and admiring circle of friends. The boy, however, remained in his torment, in the long, unending, eternal second in which his life had become suddenly and timelessly imprisoned.

There *was* no blood. A voice in his head kept telling him, there was no blood. He tried to puzzle out what it meant. What was the voice trying to explain to him? Then he realised that it was something to do with the cat, something to do with Chang. The eyes of the cat were still boring into his, but he fought against them. Gradually, he turned his own eyes again in the direction of the cat's tail, though he could not move his body. It was true. There was no blood – what did it mean?

Suddenly, the clock struck. It started to chime the twelve notes of noon. Suddenly, eternity fell away. Things happened outside, a car hooted and he heard the wind and the singing of the birds. The leaf lying on the hearth fluttered and lifted in the breeze. He could feel the sticky dampness between his legs and smell the unpleasant odour of his urine. But he did not care. With all the explosive force of an eight year old released from appalling fear, he sprang to the fireplace and seized in his trembling fingers the bits of china which had been the smashed cat's tail, turned, and ran to the door. His mother caught him in her arms and skirt.

'Give me the pieces, darling,' she said quietly, 'perhaps we shall be able to glue them together again.'

Philip Roy Lucas, 1982

BLUE-WHITE FLOWER

I was Memory, that was how I knew the place where beautiful things and sad times had come. I hung low, for my eyes refused the sun, and the city – lovely cathedral city; all dust now, and a street of dust paved unevenly. I could feel the flagstones creeping under my feet – they were worn by many journeys, the mighty had gone there, and so had the lonely. I knew they had been there, I knew the season and the hour, for my name was Memory and I remembered those things. It was spring, or part of a summer that never grew up . . .

Child: I grew up here.
Memory: In these streets, you were like grass when it was summer.
Child: Surely, under these trees I have known many changes.
Memory: You will forget what you have been.
Dream: I will remember – I have been dreaming of a skybird with a saddle for the sun to ride on, silver for the moon, a rose for the sundown, and a blue-white flower for the break of day.
Builder: Do not wander in these dreams of yours – I am strong, truly, and I will build you a palace, stone on stone, and it shall be a home for all your dreams.
Dream: Must there be so many conditions, strong one? If I wander in my dream even you will condemn me, and if I will not live in the palace you want to build, you will destroy me and there will be nothing left. Build on the people in these streets if you must, on one of the drifting lonely ones build for me.
Builder: I shall build you a palace of successes; I shall care for you all the time it takes you to understand what you must be, and I shall build, stone on stone.

Fool: Build your house upon the sand.

Dream: Let me wander on for ever.

Memory: Forever is getting shorter every moment of our life. Every second you are not checking is being passed on from you to me, and you do not even know.

Dream: Let us be joined together then, we are so much a part of one another already – only a split second divides your nostalgia and my ambition. Let us call ourselves time, for all time is the property of one or the other of us.

Fool: You are both fools.

Builder: What does it matter what you call yourselves? It makes no difference – you do not remain the same for two seconds together. I will remain; if only you would be quiet I would build you a city that would remain for ever, stone on stone.

Memory: So we've seen. All your stone on stoning has only brought you this far. The wall you've already built is too high for you to see over, and yet it is only an inch high.

Dream: It is better to be always changing – life is made of changes.

Fool: You haven't always said that, you go about clinging to things that are far more intangible than stones. You do not even know what you want.

Builder: Let us not destroy ourselves. We are together in this, and if we are strict with ourselves we shall be very strong. My city will be indestructible when I have built it, every inch I tread I will never tread again.

Memory: You move too slowly. Life isn't just stones – never has been –

Dream: Never will be – we will find more than your city in our time.

Builder: Life is beyond houses, streets (paved unevenly), beyond cities, strengths and stones. One day, strong one, you will see what I mean. For the meantime, there are the changes to come and reign among us. And out of the changes there is opening a blue-white flower for the break of day.

Angela Ince, 1973

71

THE MAGICIAN

CHAPTER I A NEW FRIEND

There was a man who lived on his own. On his birthday, he wanted to invite his friend to dinner. He thought he lived in number 22 so he walked round there and said to himself, 'I'm sure it is number 22.' This man's name was Mr K-dydydo and the man he was supposed to invite was called Mr Blab-blab-uo. He knocked on the door and a man came and said, 'What do you want?'

Mr K-dydydo replied, 'I want Mr Blab-blab-uo to come to my birthday party.'

So the man said, 'Why don't you come in my house instead?'

'All right.'

So he went inside and he asked, 'What is your name?'

'My name is Mr Palenden.'

'O, mine is Mr K-dydydo.'

'Would you like some dinner?'

'Yes, please,' Mr K-dydydo said.

'Shall I lay the table for you?'

'No need to, sir.'

CHAPTER II A MEAL WITH HIS FRIEND

'I've got a servant with eleven arms who is called an octotri because it's got eleven arms, Octo for eight and tri for three.'

'What is his or her name?'

'It's a her, and her name is Helereener, she comes from China. Come on, Helereener lay the table please, two places please. I've got another servant, it's called meranimal because it is half human and half animal, she carries the plates in. Sit down, please. As you should have realised I am a magician, I am not just a clever conjuror, I am a real magician. Please, would you choose a soup.'

'I don't mind.'

'Then if you don't mind we will have pea soup with boiled bacon in it.' He took off his shoe and poured some soup out. Mr Palenden said, 'I'm sorry. I didn't tell you my meranimal's name, she is called Icemal, she comes from Belgium.' Mr Palenden asked, 'What would you like for your second course?'

'Whatever you've got.'

'I've got everything.'

'Then can we have stew and dumplings?'

'Of course we can, actually it is my favourite. Come on, Icemal, bring two more plates in.' He took his hat off and scooped some stew out. Then he brought out his hanky out of his pocket and unwrapped some dumplings. He said, 'Do you want to eat with a spoon or do you want to eat how I usually eat, that is with the salt and pepper pots? See, I take the tops off, and eat with the bottoms.'

Mr K-dydydo said, 'I'll eat with the bottoms of the salt and pepper pots.'

'Come on, eat up, then we will go for a ride.'

Mr K-dydydo wondered what sort of ride it would be, but he just said O.K.

Mr Palenden said, 'Do you mind having your pudding (or if you would like to call it your thirds) on the way to where we are going and I won't tell you where that is until we get there.'

CHAPTER III A TRIP OUT

Mr Palenden brought a big plate in, about the size of a dinghy, and he said, 'Get on,' so Mr K-dydydo got on and wondered how it would move. Anyway, Mr Palenden got on as well. Then he got his magic wand out and said something like this. 'Early wearly goog boob wisely move,' and the dinghy-like thing moved. It went out of the ceiling. On the way Mr Palenden said, 'I call this my air plate.'

When they were halfway there they started to go down, and Mr K-dydydo said, 'Where are we going?'

'We are going to have our pudding.'

They swooped down and they went through the roof of the restaurant and landed on an empty table. They got out of the air plate and Mr Palenden put the air plate into his pocket. I just do not know how he got it into his pocket but he did.

'What would you like for pudding?'

'I would like steam pudding and black treacle.'

'O.K.'

He went over to the waitress and got his magic wand out and said Issi Wissi wand and the waitress turned into a steam pudding and black treacle, and they ate it. It was very nice. After that they got into the air plate and off they went. Mr Palenden said, 'We are here now but we are not landing because when I say what I'm going to say there will be a flock of geese, a marvellous sight!' And so there was. Then they flew home. When they got home Mr K-dydydo said, 'I must be off now.'

Mr Palenden said, 'Come again.'

Mr K-dydydo said, 'Indeed I will. Goodbye, see you soon. Before I go, will you write your address down?'

'Certainly.'

> 22 Rosemary Pink. Sink House
> Gateway Way
> CLATON
> Scarborough.

'Thank you, thank you and thank you again. Goodbye, see you soon.'

Susan Wynn (Age 10), 1977

THE WITCH'S NEW SPELL BOOK

It was my birthday and all my witch friends had given me presents. One witch had given me a new spell book and all the spells in this book were new to me.

The next day I looked in the new book and found that some spells in this book needed some things that I couldn't get. For a moment I thought, and then I had an idea. I would make a spell to make me invisible. So I got my cauldron and some wood from my cellar. Soon I started the spell – I had collected the things I needed for this potion. Soon I had finished and had it stored in bottles.

The next day I decided to do one of the spells, so I looked in the index. I started with A and then I got on to B and there it said Bigger and Smaller, page one thousand. So I found page one thousand and looked at it and there was the heading Bigger and Smaller. I read it and it said one jam tart, one of the King's boots, one knife, one fork and a spoon. I went to my potion cupboard and found some bottles labelled invisible potion. I took one of these bottles down and drank some of the potion. In seconds I was invisible and then I set out to collect the things that I needed.

First I called on the Royal Palace. When I got there I soon found the King and when I took his boot off there was a funny smell coming from his sock. Next I went to the bakers and got a jam tart, then, last of all, I went in one of the houses and got a knife, a fork and a spoon. Soon I was back in my cottage in the wood. Again I got out my cauldron and then I lit the wood under the cauldron. First I put some water in the cauldron, then I put the boot in, then the jam tart and then the three pieces of cutlery. After I had done this I started mixing the potion, looking at the instructions from time to time.

Soon it was ready and I was putting it in my potion cupboard. In the book it has two rhymes written in it, one to make the potion make you bigger, and one to make you smaller. So every day I made different potions until I had done every potion in the book. Then I thought I could have some fun with the potions I had made so I went to my potion cupboard and got out a bottle labelled Bigger and Smaller. I took the lid off and drank all the potion, then I said the magic words:

> Dogger Degger Digger
> Let me grow much bigger

and immediately I was enormous. Soon I set out for the town. When I got there I frightened all the people and they went into their houses. When I got back I said:

> Lim Lem Lain
> Make me my own size again

In a flash I was my normal size again. That night I went to all the houses and put some Bigger and Smaller potion in each of their clothes. Next morning I wrote lots and lots of letters to all the people in the town. I wrote the magic words to make you bigger to all the small people and the magic words to make them smaller to the big people. Then I made myself invisible and went to the town. When I got there I pushed each letter through the right letter-box. Soon everyone was reading the letters and when they read them the potion began to work. They looked very funny. So every day I played a trick on the town people. I did this until one day some soldiers came. Quickly I slipped some invisible potion in my pocket because I knew what the soldiers had come for. Soon they were knocking on the door. When I opened the door they yanked me up and took me to prison. I didn't care because nearly as soon as I was in prison, I was out again. When they put me in I said to the man in charge of the prison, 'Please will you come here.' When he opened the door I quickly took a drink of the invisible potion and got out of the prison without being seen. Quickly I went to my cottage, got my things and went out of the area.

Phillip Sheldon (Age 8), 1980

EXPERIENCE

MEMORIES

Old man sitting at your door
Do you wish that you'd done more?
Having reached three score years and ten
Did you rise above all men
Seeked out mountains, there to climb
Stretched to bursting that active mind?

You tell your tales of blood and war
The more they're told, the more the gore
You live on memories of what
The younger generation scorn
It gathers momentum with each telling
The dead piled high the trenches filling
Of Flanders, Somme, the glorious years
Nothing compares, unremembered fears.

You most certainly forgot
Our once grand nation
No longer great, just a blot
That Empire that you fought to save
Where many fell, some just afraid
Of going to that massive grave
The Unknown Soldier, in your heart
He was your pal, right from the start.

As you look back, nothing has bettered
That time when you felt quite unfettered
Wives and sweethearts all at home
Suffering, your fate to them unknown
No instant media, as today
Flashing in instants where battles lay
Sometimes weeks before we knew
Were you one of the lucky few.

When you have chance to reminisce
Repeat with gusto, oh such bliss
If we were unaware of mystery
You would almost create History
If we could unaware remain
We could not penetrate, lay bare
The legends created so long ago.

Some think you just survive
To keep those memories alive
The young they laugh, sometimes poke fun
About those battles, fought and won
But if it once became their turn
You'd think the act of war they'd spurn
Is it peace that they demand
Could they stand up to Command

Or in your ancient eyes just led
By your compatriots long dead
Calling from beyond the grave
We have no honour left to save.

Maybe it takes your certain courage
For them the idea is to discourage
Are you hero or a fool
Should they decline to be the tool
For politicians, statesmen, kings
Used as pawns, thought of as things
That in your time that game to play
You never questioned just went their way?

Whatever happens, dear old man
Those distant years your whole life's plan
Made you happy, gave you strength
To enjoy your life throughout its length
To sit there, ponder, reminisce
Finish your life in perfect bliss.

Elizabeth Sorrell, 1976

VISITING VENICE IS VERY WEARING

Whenever I go abroad on a sunshine holiday I always make two rigid rules, the first being to wear as little as possible and the second is to exert as little physical energy as possible. Needless to say, these two rigid rules never last very long. Why? Because the crafty tour operators make sure that the entrance hall in every hotel is plastered with advertisements for 'Not to be Missed' excursions.

Last May found me in Cattolica, lazing in the Italian sun and over-indulging in superb Italian food; it was three days after arriving that I had an unfortunate collision with the notice board which had been strategically placed outside the dining room so that guests could see how simple it was to commit physical and financial ruination: however, I was determined to completely ignore any temptations, but in my haste to walk past the object, I fell straight on top of it. The scene which followed was of utter chaos, with yours truly sprawled out and surrounded by very unsociable drawing pins plus numerous adverts for excursions, one which strongly advised me to take a day trip to Venice, so I thought the best way of apologising to the representative for my demolition of her notice board was to book for the Venice trip. After all, I always wanted to know why some idiot had left home centuries ago and allowed his bath to overflow; also why hadn't there been any qualified plumbers available to keep the drains clear, although I think it was a family affair – probably the plumber's brother was a redundant gondola builder, possibly flooding Venice was the only chance he had of making a living.

The next morning I was forced to get up at the most uncivilised hour of 5.30 a.m. in order to walk to Cattolica Square and pick up the coach for Venice. It was very peaceful walking to the Square mainly because the only two moving objects at that hour of the morning were myself and the hairdresser's dog, who was a very randy mongrel of ill-repute. At 6.00 a.m., the coach arrived, the door was flung open revealing a rather well-built female. I don't mean well-built in a sexual sense, more built to last, like a Land Rover or a Centurion tank. Nationality? Danish or Swedish; the facial expression was not very welcoming as I clambered on board – in fact I feel sure that she was a distant relation to the hairdresser's mongrel.

As with every previous excursion one had to suffer the boring and tedious routine of collecting guests from numerous hotels before even beginning the trip. After leaving the fourteenth hotel we finally started for Venice. The journey was very long, very uninteresting and extremely rough, due to the fact that the coach driver fancied himself as a poor man's Graham Hill and frequently went around corners on two wheels.

It was noon when we arrived in Venice; well, to be honest we weren't exactly in Venice but in a vast coach and car park where there seemed to be a representative for every country in the world. Our guide informed us that we must now leave the coach and get on a water-bus, making sure that you get off at Station 20. I suppose that the only way I can describe the scene where you try to get on a water-bus is as pure hell, thousands of hot, impatient tourists trying to get on about fifty buses.

After running the risk of either being pushed into the canal or trampled under foot by the madding crowd, we finally arrived at Station 20 right bang in the middle of the commercialised confusion known as St. Mark's Square, immediately being pestered by little men selling colour slides and postcards printed in Japan. The guide then instructed us to eat our packed lunch in a nearby pavement café, providing everyone was prepared to pay roughly 50p for a lager. Only thirty minutes would be allowed before the conducted tour began. Funny, it doesn't take long to be made to feel like a human sheep, with the guide playing the part of a power-drunk shepherd; this particular specimen was no exception. I, for my part, developed an overwhelming desire to push the lady into the Grand Canal, but decided not to, as some heroic fool might try to rescue her.

Lunch over, we were told to follow her and do not get lost within another party. It was obvious that our guide had gone into training for this day because, despite the heat, she managed to maintain a pace which could easily equal the four-minute mile.

On reaching the Square in a state of exhaustion, we were then told we would visit a glass-works. Inside, a spiral staircase took us down to the basement where a large Venetian glassblower was demonstrating his craft. My imagination made me wonder what might happen if the gent sucked instead of blew; possibly he would end up with a cut-glass hernia. After several boring and very hot minutes, we were escorted into the showroom to make any purchases from the large selection on display. I waited for everyone to buy what they didn't need until, at last, our guide took us outside again. Much to my relief she stated that we could have two hours free time, before departing.

I spent the time sitting in the Square under constant aerial attack from the pigeons and drinking the most expensive tea in memory – it worked out at about 25p per sip, even without sugar. As I looked around I couldn't help feeling annoyed that we, the tourists, and them, the moneymakers, had transformed a place of obvious beauty years ago into a commercialised rush hour – thousands of people, nearly all of whom were only there just to say, 'We went to Venice.' My personal opinion is that the whole outdated crumbling mess should be demolished, then rebuild everything in dazzling white stone and marble, using mirror tiles on the floor of the Square with white tables and green chairs, thus giving the total effect of a living water-lily pond. I feel sure this would bring Venice back from its present stagnation.

With the sight of our guide rushing towards me I knew that the two hours of normality were over. Everyone gathered around her all carrying various amounts of plastic trash. Her next moneymaking idea was – Anyone want a trip on a gondola? I knew when I agreed to this that I was pushing my luck beyond logical limits. Another high speed walk brought us to a smelly back alley where the gondoliers were waiting for our money and our lives. On stepping into the feeble craft I could see my whole future going the same way as the *Titanic*. Obviously the vessel was safe, altho' it's the only time I've actually seen woodworm wearing life-jackets, and it's not true that all gondoliers sing – the one we had hardly had enough breath to operate the pole. If he had tried to sing as well, it could have been fatal as well as pathetic.

After twenty or so minutes of riding in a gondola I realised that the only way to describe the experience was that one had the feeling of a small cherry on top of an oblong trifle which hadn't quite set. Onward we slowly glided around narrow waterways until we came out into the middle of the Grand Canal. This was very different, with craft of every size and shape going in various directions making our hollowed-out QE2 wobble alarmingly. It was then that I spotted a high-powered police launch coming towards us, causing a great deal of swell behind it; after just passing our gondola an extremely large wave hit us and I received a free cold shower of genuine Venetian water which was of an unusual odour, which I doubt would ever catch on as an after-shave lotion. Now, not wishing to give this story a pornographic tone I will not say where most of the water came to rest, sufficient to mention that I sincerely trusted that my legs and other parts would not turn green.

Soon we arrived at the landing stage where, with the added weight of water, I clambered ashore hoping that we had arrived at the coach. Unfortunately, our gondolier's sense of direction had gone rather astray and we were at least a mile in the opposite way to the coach park. The guide just looked at me and said, 'You follow, I know short way.' It is not at all easy trying to follow a super-charged guide when your lower regions are under flood. Half an hour of walking brought us no nearer to the coach although the heat of my body was helping to dry me out a little – it is rather nerve-racking to see steam coming from your trousers.

As Venice is full of canals, it is obviously also full of bridges; all have steps up one side and down the other. Having now just crossed the twenty-third bridge without falling once, I was seriously considering myself for the Grand National – after all, I could probably move even faster on a cool day and with dry legs. It was seventy minutes and thirty bridges later that we finally reached the coach. I slumped into my seat feeling very hot, very damp and completely shattered, especially when I heard we had walked past the coach park three times, thanks to our daft guide; not saying a word I gave that female an extremely long and unpleasant look.

During the six-hour return coach journey, we were supposed to stop for an evening meal at a roadside restaurant. However, as the owner had decided not to open that day, everyone went hungry. Personally I was past caring about food, the only ambition I had left was to reach my hotel bedroom while there was still a chance of making a recovery to my previous good health.

As the clock in Cattolica Square struck midnight I dragged my battered frame from the coach and told the guide that I sincerely hoped we would not meet again – not because I wanted to be unpleasant, but I felt sure that another excursion with her could prove fatal. With physical and mental fatigue covering me like a wet blanket, I ambled through the deserted streets, noticing that my trousers had now gone stiff; it felt as if I was walking inside a large cardboard carton.

It had been a very long day but as I turned the last corner of this marathon, there, sitting on the pavement, was the hairdresser's mongrel who gave me a cheerful welcome. At the entrance to my hotel I bent down and patted this canine casanova and offered him a little advice. If you intend to continue touring the bitches of this town, lad, whatever you do, do it locally, because, believe me, visiting Venice is very wearing.

Owen Davies, 1974

I LEARN TO BOW

Polarized I was paralysed
Plausibility palated.
People realised totally,
Woefully once I totally opened their eyes.

This is my first poem, my first breakthrough from my silent world.

I PEER THROUGH UGLINESS

Years dead tears, peter down my face,
Lucifer quietly plays me down,
Out of a light there came Christ Divine,
Peace always comes reigns awhile.

Day after dawn raw quiet rested there as I peered through
Rough pastures dew drops glistened in golden buttercups.

*I typed that poem because every day I realised more and more how
handicapped I was.*

Christopher Nolan (Age 11), 1977

DELUSIONS OF GRANDEUR

The Duke adjusted slightly frayed cuffs, consulted his watch, whistled softly. He picked up a cane. Nearly time to go into the grounds. Glancing at the old dog asleep by the hearth, he chuckled.

'Fifty-seven varieties.' Had he overheard that remark once as the animal trotted obediently behind him on one of the days when the grounds opened to the public? Really, his visitors could be quite amusing at times.

He felt in the pocket of an ancient comfortable coat. 'Sweets, most important.' The large tin stood on a shelf next to an empty bottle which had once held quite passable whisky. He lifted the lid and smelt appreciatively the delicately elusive flavour of mint toffees. Now only a few sweets rattled about the cold complacent viscera of the container. He stuffed them into the right-hand pocket of his coat, decided to leave the dog peaceably asleep, walked slowly down a passage and let himself gently out of a side door.

His slightly unsteady feet crunched on the pebbles shining palely before the gates. For the third time that week the Duke peered at the heraldic devices on either side of the entrance to the grounds. He made a minute inspection of the wrought-iron.

'Very pretty, very pretty.'

The black paint, newly sprayed, winked back at him as it reflected the rays of a watery winter sun. A good idea to get that work done before the really bad weather set in and the season came to an end.

He noticed the litter bins just inside the gates. They were an eyesore. But necessary, of course. People were becoming increasingly careless of property.

'But they must have their comforts,' he thought paternally with the ever-recurring relief that the 'usual offices' were much further away and far less obtrusive than litter bins, cafeterias and amusements. Sounds from the latter could be heard all over the home pasturage.

The old coat flapped a little against his thin legs. He lifted the cane and pointed it towards a willow enveloping a small island and overhanging a languid stream.

Should he landscape that a little better next year? Were ducks still popular? He listened to their raucous cries and rather doubted it. There were very few people about today.

The sudden click of woods made him start. He peered through a convenient gap in a high hedge and smiled contentedly. How many 'stately homes, open to the public at twenty-five pence a head' had a bowling green? Most important to add to one's revenue in every possible way. Money so short. He could see the House from where he stood between the bowling green and the stream. Badly in need of renovation and redecoration both inside and out otherwise he would never be able to stop the dry rot.

He sat down heavily on a green-painted bench and looked shyly at a well-built young woman resting at the other end, her finger in a book and her mouth pinched up in a stifled yawn.

'What's the matter, don't you fancy the amusements?' She quite looked the type who would.

She shot him a hostile glance. 'At my age?'

The Duke thought sadly of the enormous expense of installing the helter-skelter. He considered the swings and the roundabouts. What else had been imported over the past few weeks?

'At the far end of the amusement park we have a few animals in a special enclosure.'

'Oh, do we?' She accentuated the last word unkindly and looked down her nose at his cracked boots.

He noticed the thick thighs straining against the cheap black material of her skirt. 'Not a nice young woman,' he murmured to himself. Then, guiltily, 'But how much I owe to these people.'

If only it wasn't so difficult to converse these days. He tried again.

'They do a nice line in teas.'

She closed her book with a snap. Did he want to take her to tea? She didn't fancy it. A fat lot of good her getting the day off from work if Sid wasn't going to turn up. She wished he'd appear and rescue her from this annoying old bloke who seemed to take such a proprietary interest in the place.

She rose hurriedly, brushed down her skirt with a none too clean hand and tried to make her voice sound affable.

'Yes, well, I really must be off.'

The Duke rose courteously to his feet. 'No, no. Don't you come with me.' She gave a high-pitched giggle. 'Might go somewhere where you can't follow, mighten I?'

He watched her teeter away in the direction of the tea rooms. She did not look back. The Duke reflected ruefully that it was a good thing that he loved the House and grounds so much that he was willing to put up with such an invasion for the sake of sorely needed cash.

Slightly ashamed of such thoughts he picked up his cane and thrust his fingers into one of his pockets. His hand closed over the mint sweets. They were getting soft. He had not been able to stroll about the grounds in this intimate way for some considerable time due to bad weather and bad health. It felt good to be out again in spite of everything.

Perhaps if he made his way to the children's joy-rides he could unburden himself of the mints. Then back to the House for a little supper in the private apartments. He thought of the old dog, the log fire ready to respond immediately to a kindling match, the felt slippers and his latest book. Perhaps he would sit with his finger in the page just like that girl did and make pictures in the fire, the logs crackling, spitting out their vicious coruscant sparks.

Feeling a slight ache in his limbs due to the unaccustomed exercise and the coldness of the weather he rather thought that the pictures in the fire would be his evening occupation. One of the consolations of old age was to be able to rest after effort without guilt.

He hurried, tapping the cane across the grass. The miniature train would be returning from its tour soon.

The Duke stationed himself at the end of the run. The size of the crowd here was quite consoling. Some looked at him curiously. The Duke, however, felt that his battered clothes were a sufficient safeguard against being recognised. He smiled at those of his visitors who thought to smile at him and stepped forward to give an approving pat to a solitary child who carefully folded a sticky ice-lolly paper and put it in a litter bin before sucking noisily.

The train arrived. Children disgorged on to the platform. A stout woman grabbed her little boy and began fussing with his scarf and gloves.

The child looked extraordinarily handsome. 'And very patient,' thought the Duke. He took a mint from his pocket and held it between finger and thumb.

'Would you like this, my boy?'

Blue eyes sparkled and the child held out an exploratory finger. Before he could touch the mint his mother snatched him away. She glared at the Duke. He regretted deeply that for once he stood bare-headed. It might have eased the situation if he could have raised his hat to her.

The Duke smiled timidly. 'Did he enjoy the ride?'

'I suppose so.' She finished fastening the coat over a bulky scarf. 'All the same if he didn't, still costs as much.'

The Duke spread his blue-veined hands deprecatingly. 'Rising costs, death duties.' He felt a sudden urge to confide in her. To make contact after so long with another human being who was not in uniform.

'You see, I own all this.' His frail arm described an uncertain circle in the air wide and taking in the helter-skelter, the train and the animal enclosure. 'It wasn't like this in the old days before crippling taxes hit the peerage. Then we had carriages, stables, tennis courts.' His old eyes misted over. He trembled with excitement. 'Yes, in those days all was parkland, as far as the eye could see.'

He had involuntarily grabbed the woman's arm as he spoke and now became aware of a curious disturbance. She had the child protectively by the elbow and tried angrily to release her own wrist. Several people moved inquisitively towards them.

'Won't somebody 'elp me?' She shouted crossly. 'You can see 'e's crackers.'

The young uniformed driver of the miniature train came forward pushing his way gently through the small knot of interested spectators. 'Now madam, what's the trouble?'

He glanced at the Duke who stood shaking in the greatest perplexity. Perhaps he should not have identified himself or at least done so less abruptly. The lower orders were prone to inexplicable 'turns'. He studied his cane in embarrassed silence. Thank goodness John was here to deal with the situation.

The driver, whose name was Len, drew the woman to one side. The Duke caught the words, 'Lonely old codger. Harmless.' And thought that he really must do something about familiarity and blatant disregard for truth among his employees.

He watched the woman walk away. A very pleasant little boy. The Duke turned to the driver and smiled. 'Much business today, my man?'

Len touched his cap. 'Quite good, Your Grace, bearing in mind the time of the year.' He noticed the old man stagger a little. 'Are you sure you wouldn't like to go in now, sir? Most of the visitors will be leaving shortly.' He took hold of the thin arm.

'Thank you, John.' The Duke accepted help nobly and the two men walked across the grass, along by the bowling green hedge, past the litter bins and out of the wrought-iron gates across the pale pebbles.

The driver of the children's train steered the Duke gently to the right. He opened the wooden gate of a large house long past its prime, stood back respectfully to let the Duke pass. They went up an uneven garden path to a side entrance. The Duke put his key in the lock. Len gave him his cane and turned to leave.

'Just a moment, John.' The old man fumbled in his pocket, joyfully aware of the dog's panting welcome behind the door. 'Here's a shilling for your trouble. Your father spent a long time in the Family's service.'

The driver's hand closed over his empty palm. 'Thank you, sir.' He smiled the sly smile of the collaborator. 'Here's hoping the old days come back soon, sir.' He turned down the path. Pity about the Old House. Badly in need of a lick of paint. Missing a woman's hand now, of course, and surrounded by jerry-built flats.

He clattered down the path. It would be a relief to lock up the park for the night, take off his heavy boots when he got home and snatch a bite to eat.

The Duke closed the door feeling the rough texture of the dog's tongue against his fingers.

He went into the kitchen, tossed his mint sweets into the echoing tin, fetched the cheese and tomato sandwiches under cover in the larder, put on the kettle, placed his shoes in the corner, put on his slippers, found his book, used the bellows on the freshly kindled logs and settled down contented to watch the pictures in the fire.

Maureen Carr, 1975

BEFORE THE MORNING

Arranged with ritual precision,
I lie,
Motionless, tranquil,
Adequate.
There is no disability now,
No sense of urgent movement
That cannot be accomplished.

An urban silence
Absorbs the rhythmic inhalation
Of my breath.
My metabolism functions perfectly;
Only my limbs are paralysed.

I exhale gently, peacefully
As through my window
I am bathed in sodium solitude
In whose colour the world ought to be washed bland.

Yet it is not so
For there is life in this immobility,
No deficiency now,
No striving for the unreachable,
No reliance on another's hand.

I need nothing,
I am sufficient –
Before the morning.

Hilary Stevenson, 1982

PERANGAMO

Mankind meditates on lovely tear making manners in other peoples . . . Merimba rode towards Mesazem, and Merimba rode in a mad Red Bed Mercedes motorcar. Map markings placed Mesazem on a Roman boreen amid Roman toll gardes. An everlasting murky grey beastly cloud followed the fast moving car as it sped all dangerously to Mesazem. Merimba looked at the rich, coloured, foliaged green verdure thoughtfully, looked at mad game scatter in ferocious mad panic, and catapulted maniacally ahead.

Merimba Perangamo, a lustful lout to all who saw manliness as a desirable trait in a young man, meant more to his gorgeous wife than money or manliness could manage to provide. Merimba always meant more to Ruth, all paralysed, as she calmly sat passez, accompanied carelessly by a red-faced, ribald, wine swallowing, foul-mouthed woman. Ruth Eshuba, to her parents, rose all their hopes to rosy heights. All Ruth asked from her parents dearly came to her. She, in a way, found her parents' love stuffy and longed for freedom. That day came when fate attracts a soul towards its destiny, she learned to her cost.

Morning broke forth in golden marble-decked skies, a beautiful peaceful cemetery; a dear soul, alone, stood heedlessly, staring at a freshly made, brutal, brown grave. Merimba Perangamo, seeing far away from him, a lone, hunched figure, found fresh fear creeping through his fuzzy, very dead, dark, lonely dawn. Merimba looked away. Bastard that he seemed to be, he still could not approach a mad, frightened, but seemingly dead girl. Praying – something he frowned on greatly – joining grovelling, honest hands and with zealous, dilatory tears going pouring loosely, sadly, down his face, he approached, dreading fiercely his coming gory revelation. He made faltering footsteps, loose limbs lagging lazily, non co-operatively behind.

Merimba Perangamo placed some flowers in an open, shaky, very cold hand, and looking sorrowfully into lamb-sad, amber eyes, he said, 'Naught can dare aspire to make earnest my honest obligation to help you, Ruth.'

'Generations may all be buried in burial grounds,' announced Ruth poignantly, 'but my map points to this sole grave.'

Merimba laid great emphasis on his next words. 'Ruth,' he said, 'My aim, realise, is sadly, solemnly to declare candidly my part in placing you in such a tragic position. A dark night it eventually turned out to be, giving fast driving, dreadful foolhardy challenges. I made a decision to try scaring your father and mother with my daredevil driving. Recognising their red car with its familiar number plate driving carefully towards home, I frenetically found myself going more foolishly fast than usual. Narrowing the gap between us I drove hussar-like round in front of them, meaning to rev fiercely, swiftly, getting out of their path. All God's goodness could not help face my car straight rapidly. The suddenness of the fierce fright caused your father to swerve too sharply, striking the ragged fence and careering panic stricken to a ferocious death on the rocks and water in the gorge below. Pulling my car to a very deliberate halt, I numbly geared badly shaking legs to bring me down to the felonious death gorge. Unfortunately fire engulfed their car, leaping demon-like into the night.'

Looking ghastly, ambling blindly, Merimba staggered away from the scene looking carefully for any give-away surface marks on part of his car. Moaning, amounting to malapert permanent tombs, reverberations flowed from passion and great gloom in his heart. Merimba Perangamo knew an awful mad moment of sheer riveting panic. Good parents, breeding and mercy forgotten, his main aim was to make a quick getaway.

A mottled, milky, mean man reached Mullaserra, all weak, disturbed, sweating pools of mental poison. Merimba Perangamo, all mad, went towards the bar in his beautiful mansion, poured himself a large whisky and mental oblivion looked nigh.

No peace could erase Merimba's mounting leopard-spotted damnation. He all anxiously appeared to Ruth at the cemetery and gabbled greedily into lonely, moribund, all-lost eyes. All Merimba moaned about, Ruth amounted a passing summary dumb silence. She feared feelings of doom and moaning all mournfully she groped her way from the cemetery.

Merimba Perangamo made his lonely way home, fighting madly maddening undercurrents of electric thrombosis in his brain.

Merimba gave lots of thought to his next excuse for seeking Ruth Eshuba. Poor Ruth cried fulsome, dolorous tears; each passing night brought fond poor memories flowing longingly. All saw why Ruth looked dreadfully tawdry, nobody more so than her boyfriend Merimba. He only could dare hope to annihilate all looming yearnings to follow after her father and mother. Full pardon came, amending relations between two enigmatic, old fond friends. Ruth Eshuba pardoned all guilt in Merimba; she allowed friendship slowly to mature dynamically again.

Goola poached all amenities sprouting yams, old land amounting practically poor livelihood to Merimba, allowed pesetas to Goola from the sale of yams. Goola mapped moles knolls and allowed males for mating to go free. All other females were set free too. The remaining moles fetched lots of money for Goola, as their pelts were much demanded by Parisian fashion houses. Lots of money meant lots of problems, for drink was poor Goola's damnation. All his earnings bought bottle upon bottle of galvanising drunkenness. How a man remained alive living a lonely gambling with alcoholism. Life posed a yearning wish to help in Ruth's heart.

Ruth Eshuba, all sad, lopped a lot of drooping branches from a rose tree in front of her comfortable country cottage. 'Man certainly comes close to God while working with nature so lovely,' she said. Ruth took no joy no longer in gardening, but already dolorous thinking was losing ground and fresh happiness had begun dexterously, silently, peacefully, ominously, to solve her problem. As she worked she heard Merimba's fast car draw to a lightning halt. He climbed all hurriedly over the fence and lovingly, ceremoniously, came towards Ruth. Embracing Ruth he declared his special devotion and there in that idyllic setting he persuaded Ruth to marry him.

Though Merimba meant everything to Ruth she ignored an early, all-serious marriage. Calmly she went to Mesazem to work in the old parents' beautiful pastry shop. Merimba, an architect and artist by profession, very dejuvenated, smoked a great deal and dreamed his life away.

As some accounts yielded, the forlorn lame mad man lost his life going to Mesazem to Ruth's pastry shop to collect a supply of grand, home-made bread. Goola Demara found sure, kind friendship during long, all gad-about, tame months, through his friend Ruth. A door closed peacefully that Saturday in Ruth's shop. She came from the drowning-with-lovely-smells kitchen to serve her next customer. Merimba looked very handsome in his linen suit. The brashness of the blue summer shade heightened the lovely golden hue of his skin. 'Some lofty prize or made it yourself?' asked worshipping Ruth. Looking along the pastries slowly Merimba annoyed Ruth by ignoring completely her happy compliment. He annoyed her still more by demanding fresh pastries, giving a curt nod, and walking purposefully out the door.

Merimba smiled ominously, harshly, suavely, as he made his way back to his car. Most nights Ruth drove home on Highway One, but on Saturday she was in a mixed-up, demoralised, despairing state which made her nervous. She chose to take the lonesome road to Mullaserra. Already it was dark and awfully windy when Ruth made her way to her car. As parking remained a problem, Ruth arrived long after dark – sad razor-sharp tired and weary at the motorcar park.

Merimba Perangamo, madness forgotten, arrived at Ruth's house only to find the door locked. Almost immediately Ruth arrived on the scene driving very ferociously. Passion obliterated, Merimba no longer teased Ruth. Love appeared strong as he kissed his lovely, listless fiancée. Amendment, and poor lonely Ruth ameliorated, had Merimba feeling on top of the world as he looked back towards Ruth's house on his parting for home.

Ruth Eshuba appeared, dashing all hurriedly from her lovely, quaint cottage. The rain which never seems to head towards ever-hot and drought-filled Egypt, pitter-pattered on Ruth's car roof as she landed at pitiful Goola's hovel. Knocking loudly good friend that she remained always – she looked through the open window to see if Goola's poor wife slovenly lay asleep. A sordid silence saluted her as she opened the door and sadly left honey and bread on the dirty table.

Merimba, all separate, lay on his bed thinking about Ruth all alone, easily awakened, appealing pitifully, longingly for her mother. Pain seemed ever-eating into her conscience as she muttered and moaned in her boiling, golden, stuttering voice. Past, sweet memories came clearly crowding back into Merimba's fond thoughts. He remembered the first time he met Ruth. It was a glorious, great morning. Birds sang sweetly, shrilly in the huge garden at the front of Ruth's cottage. As he drew near the front door he found Ruth sowing flowers in ground looking freshly dug. All sweetness came into certain smile when she greeted him. Guiding him into the house, she set off serenely to fetch her father. They all then discussed the painting Merimba was planning to do of the homely cottage.

Merimba Perangamo lost no time in asking Ruth for a date. From that fond first meeting dear love developed earnestly, gloriously between them.

'Damp around good earth makes,' thought Bakara Monat as drops dampened arid, dry, loamy clay on the fallow, all-beautiful, marvellous loud land of the Nile River Valley. All-lovely weather past years have found undermines poor idle people's livelihood. Forlorn god-forsaken peoples ferreted a scanty existence under dreadful, raging sun, as millions of gallons of delicious cool, clear water lapped wastefully on. People rose all together to allow the easel ballast roars of the water to be used to irrigate enlarged lots, allotting loose, God's dewy pearl-drops on the lassistrall, humid land.

Merimba Perangamo allowed people to tell him their gremlin gullible, hot, lurid, loose jokes, but inwardly he was a man aware of sad solace for responsible human effort in the salvation of allotments of special, all-electric powered irrigated land from which lovely lemberyinth, loquacious peoples could manage to thrive upon.

Ruth Eshuba prayed slowly, earnestly, pitiably, sadly, as she fought frightfully for her life. Low tolls to pay if death could be averted. Food was being fed intravenously, putting new life into flagging low determination. Ruth passed all delirious, deafening, growling hours each day in lonely, gazing, all-anxious silence.

Goola Demara peered poorly towards the approaching cellar towards easy all-acute oblivion. He always spoke sweetly, respectfully to Ruth, but that changed woefully the windy night when Ruth put her foot down and refused to let him get into her grey, crowded car. Each fresh cake that rested on the car seat was for customers of Ruth and had to be delivered to their homes. Goola always relied on Ruth giving him lifts so when he stopped her car that night and he was refused he became very angry – insanely angry. Putting the accelerator violently down, Ruth darted forward, striking Goola who had gunshotted himself in front of the moving car. The car furiously crossed the boisterous, daring, human, lumbering remains of Goola Demara, and finished up lying on its roof on ground fouled up by leaking, lurid, disgusting sewer pipes. Poor Ruth lay on lonely, soggy, stinking ground, all injured and unconscious, pastries and smashed cakes loose on top of her.

Bakara Monat brought the sad news to his fond munificent friend, Merimba Perangamo. Through lonely years he had told Bakara he would stand by him until river water made viable his poor plot of land.

Merimba accepted the hospital's hopeless verdict with unusual calmness. Losing no time he made beautiful plans for his marriage to Ruth.

Bells pealed, candles burned, priests' blessings given, smiling tear-stained faces turned to watch Merimba wheel his wife, Ruth Perangamo, into love and life.

Christopher Nolan (Age 12), 1978

TABLE FOR TWO

A table for two please,
With candles and view.
My partner will arrive soon,
Have you got a light?
Thank you.

Two menus please,
I'll order later.
What's the name of that tune?
Oh and waiter,
Thank you.

Two glasses of your best champagne,
Sixty-nine, or thereabouts.
Celebrating?
Our first date out;
Thank you.

It's getting late,
The sun's died away.
My bill?
Not yet, I'll stay.
Thank you.

The flames are dim,
In the soft cool wind.
My chances are slim.
Another gin?
Thank you.

The candles are out,
The music has stopped.
In my mind there's no doubt
That the next time I come,
I'll just have to order a table for one.
Thank you.

Alan Connell, 1981

CODA

Long, long afterwards he remembered how the light returned. Into the paint-box blackness of his mind a tiny silver thread came dancing, weaving, swaying, cutting the darkness into small pieces. Suddenly it stopped and held motionless like a long-held flute note. It seemed to go on for ever – he wished it would end or that the conductor would bring him in.

He was aware of the timpani somewhere in the distance beating out a rhythm that he suddenly realised, with a shock, was his heartbeat. As the light increased shadowy, amorphous figures formed and dissolved around him. Voices came and went, up and down.

'Any signs yet, Nurse?'

'Pulse still very weak, Doctor, but he seems to be holding his own.'

'He'll pull through . . .'

I must still be alive, he thought. Please God, don't let me be alive – let me be dead. He did not know to whom he was praying – just God, any God, any bloody God who would let him die. That was what he wanted; more than anything else in life he wanted death. More than he had ever wanted to play the Brahms B Flat concerto: at eighteen that had been his greatest ambition; more than he had ever wanted to make love to Ruth or to play at Carnegie Hall. More than he had longed to take his first recording to his cancer-ridden mother before she died: it came off the press on the day of her funeral.

The voices were hovering again.

'Ever heard him play, Nurse?'

'Might have done, on the radio, but it's not my kind of music. 'Fraid I'm not a high-brow.'

'He once came to play at college when I was there – superb. I shall never forget his Appassionata. I have his recording of it – one of the finest there is . . .'

The voices trailed away; the figures dissolved into the black jelly that now enveloped him and the shaking thread of light was nearly extinguished altogether.

He was back in the room in Harley Street last week facing the consultant across a wide leather-topped desk. In his mind he referred to him as the Angel of Doom. A damned expensive Angel of Doom. Why did he charge so much to sign your death warrant? The consultant sat there in an expensively cut suit, hand-made shoes, silk shirt, Thai silk tie, playing with a gold paper-knife, all bought with fees extracted from people whose death he had pronounced.

'Sorry to say . . . rheumatoid arthritis . . . unfortunately . . . stiffening of the fingers . . . helpful drugs.'

His face, his words, his clothes, the room, began to merge into one gigantic collage of doom. The bland, cream voice seemed to get louder until it drowned the noise of the traffic in the street below. Like some vast balloon his body appeared to swell until it filled every corner of the room blotting out the light from the window behind him. Suddenly, as if pricked by a pin, he resumed normal size and was apologising for the fact that he would not be able to play the piano in two years.

'Of course, one can never tell . . . there might be a break-through . . . you never know . . . and teaching can be very valuable.' A clever man, the consultant, he spoke several languages fluently, including cliché. He shook his hand and said goodbye.

Out in the sunshine he wondered why the sun felt warm and the taxis moved as fast as ever. He signalled to one – it stopped, and took him back to the Savoy.

In his hotel room he sat on the bed and looked at his hands. It was Ruth who said he ought to see someone when he started feeling pain some months ago. His knees and hips were almost a joke. 'Poor old man, how's your rheumatism today?' And then his shoulders. Oh God! his shoulders, and that horrible Festival Hall recital. *The Times* and the *Guardian* both noticed there was something wrong. 'Disappointing . . . plethora of wrong notes . . . unusual interpretation of the Liszt Sonata.'

Ruth insisted that he made an appointment to see a top specialist when he was next in London. He would put through a call to Ruth in New York when he felt better. When would he feel better? When his fingers had stiffened so much that the simplest arpeggio became an impossibility? 'Valuable teaching' – teaching – teaching – that fool in Harley Street . . . A fool, that's what he was. Perhaps he was wrong; sometimes they did make incorrect diagnoses.

Even as he thought it he knew he was a fool. He had rheumatoid arthritis in every joint; three in every finger that laughed and jeered at each black and white note on the keyboard of the Steinway in the corner of his room.

He knew that when he phoned Ruth he would not tell her the truth, not yet, certainly not yet. Of course he would have to later, but not just yet. Why, he wondered, is it so difficult to tell someone you love the truth? They are the easiest people in the world to deceive.

The nurse took his pulse and wrote a figure on the chart at the end of the bed. She was a blue and white shape that moved around the space in his head as if on wheels. He longed for the thing to keep still but it whirled and twisted and now the thin silver line was there again.

They were dancing together – flickering in the darkness without music. Thank God, there was no music . . . no music.

'Doctor, why would he do such a thing? I would have thought he had everything to live for. Fame, wealth, all the things people long for.'

'Difficult to say, Nurse. For all we know he may have emotional problems or he may feel his playing is deteriorating. Though from what I hear his performance of the Emperor last night was heart-stopping. I know someone who managed to get tickets and they said it was unbelievably moving. Apparently the audience were stunned into silence at the end before they went wild.'

Somewhere down in his stomach was pain – he was conscious of that. It seemed as if a trail of pain led from his throat down into his body. He was puzzled; it was not the pain he had been suffering over the last few months. This was sharper, crisper, fiercer – and certainly not death.

He never really knew why he slipped out of the Savoy on Sunday morning and wandered around until he saw the church. The board outside said 'Holy Communion – 11 a.m.' and people were going in – mostly elderly ladies greeting each other effusively. Some strange compulsion pushed him through the door and someone said, 'Good morning.' He sat at the back by himself, not that he found that difficult, there was a very small congregation. From a side door the choir entered behind a silver cross, two boys, three girls and six men, who made their way to the choir stalls followed by the clergy. They were eventually lost in the oppressive darkness of the church. He had no idea of the service, he was not even sure of the denomination of the church. God had merely been an expletive to him for most of his life and his parents had been agnostics.

Someone put a card in his hand with the order of service printed on it and he glanced at it as the service progressed. Really he only wanted to sit quietly but he felt he had to kneel when everyone else did.

Suddenly he was aware of the words the choir were singing; Psalm 150, Laudate Dominum, it said on the card.

Praise Him in the sound of the trumpet: praise Him upon the
    lute and the harp.
Praise Him in the cymbals and dances: praise Him upon the
    strings and the pipe.

He could stand no more. His heart began to swell and he knew he had to get out. As he reached the door a long, thin man with a long, thin voice came up behind him. 'Are you all right, sir? Can I help?'

He shook his head, words were impossible, and ran outside. He leaned against the wall, sobbing, unable to control the shaking that was taking over his body. Gradually the sobs became less violent, more gentle. His body became calm and he reached in his pocket for a handkerchief to dry his face.

He set off at a surprisingly brisk pace along the street and turned into the first chemist shop he came to.

'A bottle of aspirins, please.'

'Yes sir. What size, twenty-five, fifty, or a hundred?'

'Oh, you had better give me a hundred,' and he added hurriedly, 'They will last longer.'

Putting the bottle in his pocket he walked on until he reached another chemist shop.

A middle-aged grey-haired lady was serving behind the counter. 'Good morning, sir, lovely morning. What can I do for you?'

He hesitated. 'I have a headache. I want aspirin.'

'Certainly, sir. Would a small packet be sufficient or do you want a hundred?'

'I'd better have a hundred. I do get headaches a lot . . .'

He paid for the aspirins and almost ran from the shop. One more lot should be enough, he thought. Three hundred must be a lethal dose.

The third shop he found open was a branch of Boots – light, bright and full of hot-water bottles.

It was more difficult to speak this time. 'One – one – one – hundred aspirins, please.' He felt the chemist was looking straight at the bulge in his pocket caused by the two hundred he had already bought. 'I am buying them for a friend,' he added nervously and unnecessarily. The chemist took them from a shelf behind the counter, put the bottle in a paper bag, and handed them over. He remembered thinking how easy it was to buy the instruments of death, paid for them quickly and left. Next door was an off-licence still open; he went in and bought a bottle of whisky. Hailing a taxi he went back to the Savoy, nodded to the doorman as he entered, took the lift to his room, put the pills and whisky out on his table and poured himself a large glass.

'Doctor,' the nurse was on the telephone, 'Doctor, I think perhaps you ought to come. There seems to be some sign of life.'

Far away he heard someone shouting as if through a megaphone, 'Signs of life . . . Signs of life,' and he wanted to call back to them, 'Look for the signs of death – of death – of death,' and he dissolved into laughter that shook his body and caused him pain.

The blue and white shape was beside him taking his pulse and feeling his forehead. 'Doctor, he was moving slightly and trying to speak. I almost thought he was laughing.'

'Perhaps he was, Nurse. Let's have a look at him. Pulse is stronger. He had swallowed a lot of aspirin and whisky so is bound to take a while to recover. Strange to think it was probably the whisky that saved his life – he got drunk before he had taken enough aspirin.'

The light in his head was growing even brighter. The thin silver line had become a star that sparkled and shone and was pushing the darkness away. He could see, albeit faintly, the nurse's cap and the doctor's white coat.

'Come on, old chap,' the doctor's voice was kind and compassionate. 'You are going to be all right.'

At that moment he wanted to cry out. He did not want to be all right and alive. All right to him was death. Did they not understand? How could they be so stupid? In a few years time his hands – through which he spoke, through which he lived – would have stiffened up so much that he would be as good as dead.

'Your wife . . .' The doctor was saying something about Ruth. 'Your wife is catching the first flight on Concorde to be with you. The hotel contacted her, I believe.'

Suddenly he remembered he had written her a letter before taking the pills. As if the doctor read his thoughts he said, 'Here is your letter to her. You won't need it now. Shall I tear it up?'

He nodded quietly and the pieces of expensive Savoy Hotel notepaper fell from the doctor's hands into the hospital wastepaper basket.

Andrew M. Robertson, 1983

A BRIDGE TO UNITE

'They'll be here about eleven,' Alan Harris said as he came into the kitchen in his Saturday working clothes. 'If that's a pot of coffee which you've just made, I'd be glad of a cup.'

'Who will be here?' Paula asked as she steadied herself to pour some coffee. It was a silly question. Somehow she felt that it would postpone a bad moment a little while longer. It had hung over her now like a threatening cloud for two whole weeks, but until the words were actually spoken, they seemed to be something of a dream.

Alan dropped into a chair, his long legs stretched out in front of him. 'The tree-felling people,' he said.

So it was happening at last. Paula could not bring herself to look towards the tree; instead, she worked at stacking the coffee cups in the sink. Alan drained his cup and levered himself up from the chair – he was eager to be outside. Paula considered that he had aged a great deal, especially in the six years since their only daughter, Julie, had become married.

'How long will they take?' she asked. 'The tree-felling people, I mean.' Alan considered. 'Most of the day I should think, a tree that size must be the best part of eighty years old.'

A hundred at least, her mind told her with a pang. A whole century covered by a single tree. Alan looked at her for a moment. 'You are worried by the tree business, aren't you? Well, try not to worry too much. By the way, I asked Julie and Brian if they would like to bring young Bill round, to watch the tree come down. They will be here in a minute.'

Paula paused. 'Is it safe to have a four year old around when they are felling a tree that big?' The words choked her.

'Well, he can stay in the house until it's down and then come outside when the fun begins.'

Fun! thought Paula. Is that all they think it is? How could she explain to Alan, to whom a tree was just a tree, that to her it was a symbol of everything that had happened in their past. Now they were going to chop it down. Just like that! Paula considered that at least it would be a chance to see young Bill, because even though they lived nearby, they did not visit very often these days. Paula returned to the washing-up as she tried to control her thoughts. The morning dragged on.

It had been two weeks ago that Alan had said that the ash would have to come down – the day after the storm. They had woken to discover the lawn covered in debris from the tree. He asked her if she had heard it during the night. Yes, she had heard. They both knew it would have to come down.

Paula shivered, remembering an earlier storm when Julie was ten years old. There had been no sign of debris then. The next day Julie had been playing on the swing when the branch gave out, hurling her as it went. It had been considered enough just for the tree to be made safe then.

After Julie had come out of hospital she had never stayed at home for very long. Her legs were now completely useless. First she had gone for rehabilitation, then on to a school for people like herself; then, before she had met Brian, she had lived in a nearby centre. When they got married, the council had given her a local ground-floor flat in which she could cope. Admittedly, even with the changes they had made to the house it was still difficult to get Julie's chair around. Supposedly, this was one of the reasons why she did not come very often. Her mother knew there were others.

Thinking back even further, she thought of when they had first bought the house; Julie had been six then. Paula remembered her trying to circle the ash with her little thin arms. She also remembered her asking Alan to build the swing. And he had. He would do anything for her. It hurt him that she did not come very often, although he never said.

Paula finished the washing-up as she thought that the Julie she once knew was a million miles away, even though she only lived on the other side of the town. Paula knew she could no more have understood her than she could have climbed the willowing ash. Still, at least she was not bitter any more. If only she were not so uncaring about the old house, the garden, so critical of them for going on living there. It was not that Julie was jealous – she and Brian lived in a small modern flat with only a patio for the child to play on – but it was more than this that divided them now. It was some hidden antagonism which she just could not appreciate. Yes, the Julie she had known was definitely a stranger.

Outside there came a toot of a horn. Brian's familiar signal. Suddenly there were several unknown voices; the tree-felling men had arrived.

The kitchen door burst open and young Bill came running in. Julie gave her an impersonal kiss on the cheek. 'Now Mother, we've brought our lunch so there's no need for you to start fussing about making lunch.' Julie could never bring herself to accept anything, Paula thought, not even a meal.

'I want to watch,' said Bill, climbing on the table to get a better view from the kitchen window. 'Why don't they hurry up and chop it down?' Paula winced, but she could not expect the youngster to care. She poured some orange juice for Bill and made some coffee – at least Julie would accept that, she thought. As she made it she wondered if it really was something to do with the fact that there was no old house with an overgrown garden and trees to be chopped down that made Julie so distant. For hers was a new world, 'tailor-made' for modern living.

'You're still here, then?' Julie said as she drank her coffee.

'Still here? Of course we are still here. It's our home, isn't it?'

'You're out of touch out here, all alone. Brian is always saying it's time you found a nice little flat in the town, like ours. No garden, not so much work, then you would not have things like this tree-felling business to worry about.'

Paula paused, her coffee cup in her hand. 'Maybe you're right, but we like it here, we don't want to leave. Why, your father has never given it a thought.'

'That's his trouble,' Julie replied, 'he doesn't think. Brian was only saying the other day that he ought to have a word with him.'

Paula was stunned. 'But I hoped that you liked coming here. There is a garden for young William to play in, all the things which you used to do when you were a child. Don't you remember? We like it, your father and I, it's our sort of place.'

'Well, it's not mine,' Julie said shortly, as she moved from the table and over to the window. 'Honestly, Mum, there is nothing for me in a place like this. Oh, of course, there's you and Dad; apart from that, well, people just don't live in places like this any more. I used to like it when I lived here. You do when you're a kid. But you grow out of what you like when you're a child, don't you? It's only natural.'

Paula busied herself preparing bread and cheese lunches for the men. It was no use wanting Julie to be other than herself. But this was more than a generation gap. It was to do with the kind of people they were and the things they held dear. She looked out into the garden but dared not look at the tree. Over by the hedge she saw Brian and Alan talking and wondered if they were having the fateful conversation.

'Can I have some cheese?' Young Bill slid down from the table. 'I like cheese. They are using a big saw out there. I've been watching them all morning. Can you hear them?'

Paula could. The sound was like a bee buzzing out of her sight. 'Your Mum has brought your dinner – this is for the men.'

'You can go into the garden now and Daddy will show you what they are doing,' Julie said, as the men came away from the tree for lunch. Young William ran out into the garden, calling his father as he went.

Alan and Paula had lunch together. Alan looked tired. 'How are things going?' Paula forced herself to ask. 'Fine,' Alan replied, running a hand through his hair. 'Hard work felling a tree.' The precision involved in felling the tree appealed to his nature. 'Why don't you come and watch?'

'I didn't feel like it,' Paula said as she tried to smile. 'I saw you talking to Brian.'

'Yes, he's a nice chap, I think he is good for Julie. I just wish they would come and see us more often, but I suppose they consider us past it.'

'Have you ever thought of finding somewhere else to live?' Paula chose her words carefully.

'Funny you should mention that, Brian was only saying about it this morning.' He stopped, sitting his spoon in his coffee.

'Yes?' Paula urged him.

Young Bill burst into the kitchen and slammed the door. 'Why can't I stay outside and watch it fall down? I want to see it crash.'

Alan lifted him up and placed him on the table. 'You can watch from the window.'

'When I hear the crash can I come out?'

'Yes, you can come out then,' Alan said as he levered himself up from the chair. Patting Paula on the shoulder as he went, he disappeared into the garden.

It was midway through the afternoon. Julie had taken young Bill next door to see the animals when the confines of the kitchen table had become too much. Paula was alone. She looked out into the garden and found she could do nothing but think about the tree. It's the tree, she thought, that's the trouble. When that tree falls it will widen the divide it started several years before, this time it would fall between her and everything she loved. Her and Julie, perhaps even her and Alan. She wanted to turn away from the window but forced herself to stay. As if it had recognised its own defeat, the ash was beginning to bow a little; it resembled a prisoner that had been condemned.

Julie and young Bill returned, talking about what they had seen. Suddenly the humming of the saw was exchanged for the ringing of an axe, which rang like a death toll. Surely the end must now be near?

Paula was just about to make a cup of tea when a shout told them that it was time to go into the garden. Young Bill became excited as Julie told him that he must stay close to his dad and do what he was told. Everyone moved towards the far end of the lawn. Paula would have liked to hang back.

'Come on,' said Alan, standing beside her. 'This is something you should not miss.' As she moved towards the others Paula knew that what he said was right. For had she missed this moment, she would have missed the moment of truth!

Safe from harm's way the little group of onlookers stood in silence. Suddenly the great trunk began to quiver, then came a rending sound and a thunderous roar. With a sound like that of a wind. Sky, leaves and branches reeled in front of their eyes. With a final sigh the tree was down. It was as though the garden was in mourning for its friend. Still no one spoke, it was as if words had escaped them. Paula clung tightly to Alan's hand; as she looked up she saw that Julie's face was wet.

'That was very sad. I don't think I liked it.' The child spoke as if for all of them. Julie was strangely silent as they moved back towards the house.

'I am staying here to play. I can climb right up the tree now.' Little Bill ran as fast as his legs would carry him.

'I thought I'd forgotten about this place until the tree came down but I am beginning to see what you mean, now. That tree was part of me.' Julie talked to her mother as they watched the child play. 'Do you remember the swing? Perhaps we could find it and another tree for William to play on.'

'But I thought . . .' Paula stopped. If that was how Julie felt why talk about it? It was as though for the first time in ages, mother and daughter actually understood each other. Could it be that the tree had fallen to act as a bridge to unite, rather than to divide?

'There will be enough logs to keep us warm for a few winters yet,' Alan said as he came into the kitchen. 'Then you're not thinking of moving?' Paula suggested.

'Moving? Who's moving? This is our place, isn't it? For our sort of people.'

They all looked out of the window and each of them remembered.

Ann Trotman, 1974

THE OLD PILLAR FOR EVERY OCCASION

The pillar raised peasant hopes,
A dark past oasis parted there,
Through a street ran a rat gaunt scraggy and mean,
Opinions expressed elected panic I hear.

Parents ordered their children in out of the street,
An evil past appeared darkly there
Old years, razor sharp, rainwashed down
Appearing to frighten half the town.

The tool of treason Poland's regret,
Every order eroded, years upset,
The pillar yielded refuge, and perfect grace,
Eventually fitting a revered safe place.

I wrote that poem about the revolution in Poland. Poland could stand for any country. The pillar was a port to peace and security.

MY AMBITIONS

Taste of pity as people stare,
Love, lots of love from mother,
Pills you find as lasting prayer,
An irate person may possibly
Have faith instead of despair.

Christopher Nolan (Age 11), 1977

MILKMAN

In the auld days, just after the First World War, the milkman was chappit up at fower o'clock in the morning. It was a right racket at the door, 'Bang! Bang! Wauken up! Wauken up!' Then the soond o' the chapper's bits going on up the street. 'Same auld thing every morning,' said the milkman, as, wearing his dungarees and his bannet over his lugs, he went out tae the back yaird to feed his cuddy. The cuddy was broon and a braw horse o' seeven years auld. He brushed it doon and pit it in his cairt. Then he loaded on the muckle churns and wee pitchers. Off he went over the bumpy stanes – clip – clop!

Doon the street he met the polisman who said, 'All quiet in the toon last night – a' soond asleep.'

'Are ye away hame tae yer bed then?'

'Aye, Wullie, aye, see ye the morn, same time, same place.'

Now it's the doctor.

'Aye, Doctor! What are you daeing oot at this time in the morning wi' Jack Frost aboot?'

'Ye ken Teenie at the bottom o' the hill? Her bairn's on the way.'

'Oh, aye! That'll be Jock Tamson's wife and he'll be awa' doon the pit. I'll send me laddie for him. Here, laddie, rin and get Jock Tamson up frae the pit.'

'I'm on my wey,' said the doctor, as the laddie went hoppin' doon the street, whistlin' a sang, and without a care in the warld.

The milkman carried on with his roond and caught up with the postman. 'Aye Boab! How's the King's Mail, the day?'

'Loaded doon wi' a big parcel for Teenie and Tam. I think it's frae her mither for the new wean.'

'That's fine. The doctor's just awa' doon there noo.'

'Have you a minute to hear aboot the Robertson bairn? It was him gied the laddie Boyter a walloping. There'll be work for the polis over that eh?'

'The polisman never spoke aboot it – so he disnae ken yet, or else he didna want to speak aboot it!'

They went on their wey, and the milkman's next call was at the mansion hoose, where he expects to get a piece. If it's the auld housekeeper, he's quick aboot it. But when it's the cosy tae cuddle young maid wi the long broon hair he chats her up. (Of course, his wife doesnae ken aboot it! Or does she?)

It's the maid this morning and Wullie's face brightens up. 'How's my wee sourocks this morning?'

'Fine. Like a cup o' tea Wullie?'

'Aye and a wee cuddle with it!'

'Ooh,' she said, nudging him. 'Ye'll need to help me wi the breakfast dishes for that.'

Just then the auld housekeeper came in wi her crabby face, her grey dirty hair and her nasty tongue and he scarpered away.

The milkman reached Jock and Teenie's hoose as the clock struch seeven. The doctor was just leaving wi' a sad face. 'Puir thing, the bairn's feet are a' twisted. She'll never be able to walk. Naething I could do about it. Teenie's breaking her hert, and I didnae ken what to do or say.'

'Puir lassie, I'll have to see if I can cheer her up,' said the milkman, and he went into the garden where the flowers were braw in the rain, and on into the clean wee hoose.

'Aye, Teenie! What's this then? My! That's a bonnie wee facie.'

'It's no her face, it's her feet. They're a' twisted.'

'Wi' a face like that, dinna bother aboot her feet.'

'It's what's gaun tae happen to her when I'm not here to look after her. She'll need it all her life.'

'You'll ha'e mair o' a family surely, to look after her.'

'But Wullie, I couldn't bear to think they might a' be born with bent feet.'

'Aye, it's a queer world.'

Just then Tam came back from a walk to think things over. 'Teenie,' he said, 'I've been thinking. What aboot if you and me wait to see what happens? You see we mustn't worry now, about the day that might never come. We've just got to wait and work together. Let's start right noo and I'll away and make a cup o' tea.'

Chapper Up	Man who wakens people who have to go to work early, by knocking on their doors.
Bits	Boots
Bannet	Cap
Lugs	Ears
Cuddy	Horse
Braw	Fine
Muckle	Big
Wee	Small
Aye	Yes
Wean Bairn	Child
Laddie	Boy
Ken	Know
Piece	Sandwich
Sourocks	Sorrel leaf (to whistle through)
Braw Bonnie	Beautiful
Dinna	Don't

James Anderson (Age 13), 1977

VICTORIA ROW

I sometimes think back to my childhood
to a different world
Where our once proud house stood
In Victoria Row.
My father worked in the factory
Whose belching chimneys scared the town
Ragged children roamed the streets
and the workers trundled home.

Times were hard then
and our house was one of hundreds
built in streets, line after line
little alleyways stood between them
where we used to play
Though we were happy
in that time of long ago.

The years went by and I stayed put
and worked in the factory of my childhood memories
to think my father worked in those very walls
to earn an honest bob.
Mrs Jones still put out her washing
and the stray dogs wandered by
Smoke poured out of the factory
and the old town was all alone.

How could I know when I was young
all the changes that were to come
through wars and depressions
and joys and tears
and then the terror of the scientific sun.

The sixties came and I was happy
living out my time, at peace with the world
Most of the neighbours had gone now
and their houses were boarded up
But I was happy, and it was home
in Victoria Row.

Cardboard cities, concrete jungles
Mad planners taking over the world
'Come live in a brand new monstrosity
that in ten years will be vandalised or falling down'
Street after street the houses fell
and down with them my memories and my life
Now I'm sitting in my brand new flat
looking at the shopping centre, Victoria Row.

And now I live my life alone
except for the families above and below
the times when the elderly were respected
have seemed to vanish, far away
They are all too busy living their lives.

The daily delivery of pints of milk
and the chaotic supermarkets my only contact
with the world
Sitting here watching the rain pouring
seeing the drab, sprawling town
and a time of long ago.

Richard Mayson (Age 15), 1982

THE LONELINESS OF A SHORT STORY WRITER

I'd like to speak to you, but where do I begin? What do I say? I just haven't a clue. Some famous writers start out like this:

Brook Bond slipped his hand along her thighs as she flicked the blue chips between her vinyl smooth fingers. The marble rattled round the roulette wheel, with the croupier unable to concentrate as he attempted to tear his eyes away from her deep cleavage.

Great stuff, I thought, but I couldn't write like that. How can I when the only excitement that I have had from gambling is from a game of Housey Housey from my bed at Munrow Wood Orthopaedic Hospital.

Munrow Wood – now there's a place! How could I make that exciting? How does this sound:

My Mercedes turned into the cedar-lined drive with its hi-fi stereo playing Mantovani's 'Rhapsody in Blue' as the loose granite chippings crunched under my high-speed radial tyres. The vivacious blonde private nurse wiped my forehead with her lace handkerchief as it lay nestled against her thirty-eight inch chest. The scent of her perfume played havoc with my imagination.

The car slowly glided to a halt. The eager hospital staff were waiting in anticipation of my arrival. The door clicked open and the Kildare-like figure of the head specialist rapped out orders to the nymph-like nurses who stood staring at my pain-racked, chiselled features. 'Try to concentrate Nurse, and get off your knees. He's only human you know.'

There's a laugh! Here's what really happened. I could hardly walk up the sludgy, pot-holed path, with its steep hill which was about two miles long, from the bus stop to the hospital. And then I'd had to get off at the previous stop to the hospital because I'd only had one and ninepence instead of one and ten!

I'd come here, I thought, to have three major operations,

because I could hardly walk. By the time I reached the entrance, the handles of my brown carrier bag had ripped off and a hole in the bag where it said 'High Class Butchers' had allowed my old bedroom slippers to poke through.

It took me a good five minutes to catch my breath before I could acknowledge the invitation to 'Walk In', written approximately a hundred and fifty years ago, on the paint-peeled door. I did so, wiping away the sweat covering my face with a pair of khaki socks supplied by the Territorial Army. I could write another story about that organisation!

'Name?'

'Whose?'

'Whose do you think?' retorted the receptionist, and without raising her head she took the crumpled introductory card from my hand.

What am I here for? I began to wonder. I mean, why did it have to happen like this? How could I write like that? Why couldn't it have been like this?

The nymph-like nurses gently supported my body out of the Mercedes on to the interior sprung stretcher, gently tucking in the pre-heated continental quilt, and continually asking if I was comfortable, and arguing who was going to push me. One gave in to the other on the promise that she could do the first bed bath.

The stretcher glided us into a luxurious private room absolutely full of flowers and get-well cards. In one corner of the room a sunken ivory bath had been prepared with a fragrance of spice.

By now the nurses had revealed their names to me, and Claire gently removed my dragon-patterned silk dressing gown and Karate-style py- jamas, revealing my bronzed body. Claire and Melanie gasped and the soft white flesh of their faces turned deep crimson as they gently slipped me into the water. There I floated and through my half closed eyes, I could see my help mates squabbling as to who was to prepare the bed.

They were interrupted by a middle-aged but beautifully shaped Sister. 'Nurses, nurses!' she snapped, 'this must stop at once! Don't you realise how lucky you are, winning the competition over four hundred other girls, just to be nursing this man?' She continued briskly, 'Whilst the hospital management is grateful that you are working without pay, some nurses, you know, were prepared to give over their life savings to us just for this one occasion.'

Tears rolled down Melanie's face. 'Please forgive us, Sister, only don't take us away.'

'This is your last chance,' said Sister as she began to approach the bath.

'Be a little understanding, Sister,' I said. 'This must be a very traumatic experience for them.'

She smiled and said, 'How do you feel, dear? Are you ready to come out?'

I nodded benignly. Her manicured hand reached down for me, accidentally touching me where it wasn't necessary. I quickly covered myself over in order not to punish them unnecessarily, and I was soon in bed.

Oh, that would have been nice, if it had happened that way but the reality was: after being ushered out of the reception room I was told to go to Ward Eight; she could have said cell block eight. It reminded me of a prison camp; it was like a maze, and from the outside the different wards were shaped like Nissen huts.

I stopped two white-coated teenagers who were bespattered with blood and I thought the meat department must be quite near.

'De ye hear mate, where's Ward Eight?' They smiled and one curled up laughing. The other one replied, hardly able to get his words out, 'Second left along there.' And as I passed them, I saw the cards on their coats revealed them as doctors.

I entered, clutching my carrier bag, and was nearly knocked down by an unshaven old man in his nineties seated in a wheelchair.

Well, I thought, here I am, and at least someone is worse than I am, when suddenly a big-jowled female face (I could tell it was female because she had lipstick on) shouted down the corridor, 'Doctor McAllistair!'

The old man in the wheelchair spun round. Strewth, I thought, he's a doctor. The full figure of the woman seemed to block the corridor leading into the ward.

'Who are you?' she said, asking me the question, then speaking to the old man. 'I've found your contact lenses while emptying one of the bed pans.'

She practically pushed me into her office. 'Who's your surgeon?' she rasped, in a voice that any sergeant major would have been proud of.

'Doctor Jackson,' I said.

'He's not Doctor but Mister,' she said, rebuking me at the same time as writing my name. 'Take your things to bed 36 and get into your pyjamas.'

'Oh, Sister, I don't wear pyjamas.'

She ferreted through a washing basket and sorted out a pair of pyjama bottoms. 'Here, wear these! Mr Thomas has had his legs off and he won't be needing them.' The cheeks of my buttocks squeezed together at the thought.

'Keep your shirt on,' she ordered, 'till we get you a top. Mr Erickson won't last the night, then you can have his.'

I entered the ward which reminded me of a sailing ship, with its many ropes and strings decorated with plaster casts of arms and legs.

'But don't get into bed, you'll need a bath.'

'I've had a bath, Sister.'

'You'll have another. Sit on the chair at the side of the bed until Nurse Jones comes for you.'

I walked down the ward, looking at the numbers on the beds. 36. There was mine with curtains round. I took a peep through a gap in one of the curtains and there in the bed lay a dead man.

I felt my hair stand on end. My request for a laxative would no longer be necessary. A face appeared from under the bed and a grey-coated ward orderly looked very pleased with himself as he located the man's false teeth.

'What do you want?' he said.

'I was told to come to bed 36.'

'That stupid old bag! She knows we're laying out patient 36! She never gets off her fat . . . Look, sit on the bed next door.'

It was like sitting on a park bench. I was still feeling a little sick after the shock and at the thought of lying in a dead man's bed.

A squeaky voice of what looked like a nurse but could have doubled for Olive Oyl in Popeye cartoon, announced, 'I'm to take you to the bathroom. Slip into your dressing gown,' pointing to the one on the wall.

'It's not mine.'

'Well, he'll not need it where he's going.' Making out she knew where the dead went. I put it on and thought he looked much bigger lying on that bed, as the sleeves finished halfway up my arms.

She took me along to a room, at the end of the ward, that could have been used for chilling beef. Olive ran the bath and commanded, 'Take your clothes off, then.'

'Well . . .' I said hesitantly.

'You'll soon lose your modesty here. There are no locks on the doors, not since the suicide last year.'

I've never felt so embarrassed. The cold had such an adverse effect on some parts of the body, and one part in particular would provide a talking point in the nurses' quarters for some weeks to come. Now two people knew of my well-kept secret.

'Excuse me dear, can I just use the sink to soak these few pots?' the Jamaican ward orderly asked.

I slipped into the three inches of tepid water which was getting colder by the minute because of a draught coming through a broken window. Olive provided me with a towel and I quickly realised how a piece of wood felt when being sandpapered.

I mean, how could I write about those experiences? It would have sounded much better this way:

After being powdered down, I lay in a bed specially flown in from the USA with hydraulic bed springs. Sister Matick appealed to me, 'Is it convenient for the specialist to examine you now, D.J.?' Using a name I had allowed the staff to call me.

'Fifteen minutes, Sister, is that all right? Just while I finish this large scotch.'

I gave the specialist instructions to enter, and he appeared with his five assistants, private secretary and photographer. He requested to look at my disease, because of its rarity. I had picked it up in the Amazon jungle. I was leader of an expedition to find the lost tribe of the Tiki-Tiki, and suddenly, when I entered the tomb of Tutum Yawhawn, a poisoned dart, of which there is no known antidote, entered my thigh. I lay paralysed for months. I had made a partial recovery, but my legs had become distorted and my hands had gone white, like a leper's.

The Sister pulled back the silk sheets for an intensive examination, and looks of admiration showed on their faces for my tremendous courage.

'We've got good news, D.J.! The world's first three minute miler has offered you his legs, and the leading pianist with the London Philharmonic Orchestra his hands, so things look all set for your operation. I'd like to introduce our leading anaesthetist who will assist me.'

'But I'd like to watch the whole thing – just give me something to bite on and a couple of whiskies and I'll be all right.'

After the examination they went into the corridor where a crowd had gathered in order to catch a glimpse of me.

'Before you have a little sleep, D.J., two producers from the BBD and ITD would like a few moments with you.'

After mentioning thousands of pounds, I told them that I would not be partial and that they could both film the whole operation, with a five minute interview between legs for the BBD and between hands for the ITD.

'D.J., D.J., time to wake up!' The morning for the operation had come, and after eating eggs, bacon and mushrooms, washed down with a large pot of coffee, I prepared myself.

Melanie and Claire began to hover over me. Anyone would have thought it was my last day on earth. Telegrams from well-wishers began to pour in. I read Her Majesty's first, which she had signed with her pet name known only to us. My blood pressure was then taken with much difficulty because I was so calm they couldn't find a pulse. I was put into the sterilised dress of the hospital with my initials, D.J., on the front.

A pre-med needle appeared in the Sister's hand.

'What's that for, Sister?' I asked respectfully.

'It's to keep you calm when you go into the theatre. You may feel a little nervous.'

'Me? Nervous?' I said, and for the next few minutes I related my experiences in a Nazi concentration camp.

I kissed all three of my admirers and after the smelling salts had been wafted in front of Claire's nose, I was gently lifted on to a hydraulic trolley, and, while being pushed, one young woman had to be clubbed before she finally let go of my hand. Into the theatre I went, and as the white-coated audience clapped, I took the whisky and the operation began.

It didn't take long to take off my left leg; the audience stared in wonderment.

'How do you feel, D.J.?' the T.V. announcer asked.

I took the piece of two by one out of my mouth and said, 'Ooh, Ooh! That was cold!'

'Sorry D.J., it was your new leg out of the freezer.'

If only you could have new legs and new hands; if only these things had happened to me; but is the truth really worth writing about? This is what really happened on the morning of the operation: all the lights were switched on at six o'clock in the morning and a bowl of water flopped backwards and forwards as the night ward orderly raced round with bed pans and bottles with all the skills of a Chinese plate-balancing act, trying to keep everyone going at once.

'Wakey Wakey, number 36!'

I'd never seen six o'clock in the morning before. Afterwards the breakfast trolley sailed past my bed.

'Nothing for you, 36.'

'Can't I even have a piece of toast?' I asked, as my stomach pleaded with my mouth for sustenance.

The orderly jokingly replied, 'If you have anything now we'll only be getting it back later on.' I was later to learn that he wasn't joking.

Nine o'clock, and Olive took me for another bath, to shave my arms and legs in preparation.

'You're next after 35 in the theatre. It's just a simple cartilage operation.' I'd already seen two simple cartilage operations and their after-effects.

Ten o'clock came and 35 returned looking like an aqualung diver, with a clamp holding his tongue and a pipe up his nose. The shaking of my legs began to inform me that I wasn't one of the brave ones of this world. The pre-med needle quickly dried my mouth, but it stopped my legs shaking. It must have been the truth drug, because I began to express myself with all my inhibitions gone. Olive could have won the Miss World contest! I felt great, but I could hardly move my legs.

It was snowing outside as they pushed me through the corridors in a wheelchair, into a small room where the anaesthetist was waiting with a large needle which he pushed into the back of my hand. The next thing I knew I was back in the ward with a large cage over my legs, and the television was on full blast with the music of *Rawhide*. I'd never felt such awful pain and I began to remember the way I had spoken about people who committed suicide. Never again! I had begun to wish I was dead and a feeling of sickness began to overtake me. That night was the longest I have ever spent, and the next morning I just managed to look down to my legs which were encased in plaster and covered with blood.

Visiting time arrived with my wife telling me how lucky I was to be in such a warm bed with the snow a foot thick outside and my mother had brought me a bottle of orange juice.

'I think they've took my feet off,' I said to them, 'and the pain's killing me.'

My mother who had never been sympathetic, probably in order to toughen me up, said, 'Don't be so bleddy mardy,' as she quickly downed the grapes that my wife had brought me, which she could hardly afford as the holes in her bootees was a witness to.

'The Electricity Board's been and cut the electric off, and the washing machine's been taken back,' my wife reminded me to add to my miseries. 'I couldn't pay them anything out of your six pounds nine shillings sick pay. And I've been thinking, duck, if you can get the almoner to lend you ten bob, I can bring three of the children to see you next week.'

'Well, we don't have to bother about that, I'm coming out next week. They've told me they need the bed.'

Miserable, isn't it, but should my story end like that? The story writer would have ended it by writing:

After having his hands and legs replaced by transplant, D.J. stood up, looked into the tailor's mirror and said, 'Beautiful job.' And as he walked back to his private room, amid the cheers, a surprise was waiting for him. For who should greet him but his old friend, with his full orchestra, James Last, minus his pianist.

'Sit here, D.J.,' and for the first time in D.J.'s life he played the piano.

What a way to end a story.

David J. Swift, 1980

DO YOU?

Lunatics nearly nominated madness,
Normal nebulae broke feignedly through,
Menfolk munched on brittle traithnins,
Nodding women snored and cauterized,
Mentioning, I don't believe it, do you?

COULD YOU?

Bernadette breathed beauty on lonely boyhood,
Nought was wanted in gloriously rendered main,
Could you imagine me, seeing and noting many
Mundane images, which moved hither and thither –
In my mind, no longer normal, they became
Magnificent notions and consequently,
My harried brain leaned downward on my chest,
Thinking, memorising, repeating, listening
In my ear for the effect of my words,
I realised my munificence of knowledge,
I endangered my freedom of expression
If I did not disembowel my notorious madness,
In impeccable language, agonisingly written,
In numerous, tantalising, spasmodic-ridden
Onslaughts, on a rickety, moaning typewriter?

YOU COULD?

Newman said nobody is their brother's keeper,
Aquinas said candour in belief cannot be negative,
Centuries lovingly lustred lonely mystics
    mental diadems,
Ireland lengthens her benign dangerous
    nefarious assumptions,
Could access to nullifying nemesis, venially
    mummify pentateuch,
Could easy nuggets be sampled freely,
    negatively, newly,
Mammoth, notable, immediate, vexed questions
    bear answering
Census point to new heady awareness in cloistered
    irrelevancy,
Could you imagine nothing of God in the
    wonderful future – you could?

IF YOU?

Vellum balls benign-men made,
In knowledge made benign,
Cunning men must not –
Become, bold nor benign.

Beauty cares not on whom
She falls, bother thinks
Likewise too, mental agility
Beckons at youth's
Numbest candidate too.

Nothing can chill the –
Nectar neat in bee's
Noble mead, caves-men
Noted increasingly cutely,
How marvellously lasting bee's breed.

Nothing dangerous can ever fan
Celestial-breathing benignity,
Much beneficent tellings
Centuries moodily nestle with dignity.

Benedictions blew between
Sanguine men, cautioning
All of them to bear, their
Cross in beautiful certainty,
Finding ease, at the well of care.

Nursing neat awareness
Unlikely before, all eager
Took hope entow, and vanquished
And loser voiced love's delights,
And voiced caution no more.

Naught were the nemesis –
Centuries cascaded on,
Another day had dawned,
Seeming weakly in despair,
Calming influence lingered there.

Bending certainty endemically,
Beastial address melted through,
Bold enterprise bonded meekly –
Null and mournful, battening menfolk
Announced, 'I Rabbi, if You let me,
Will sweetly feel as You?'

TRY?

Christ's news came neatly –
Packed, in beautiful vales
Of tears, melting snow white
Bends in the verdant, nigh
Azure-blue vaults of the
Firmament, freeing numerous,
Countless samples of benign
Faith, in God's cool, clear
Waters of sweet, sparkling,
Clam-like, death-defying
Sustenance, succulently supplied –
In heady, delightful, denim-lasting
Franchise, upon the Altar of Love.
No longer could cedars credo
Asleep, no longer could numbness –
In feelings be heard, nobody
Feared all mesmeric doubt,
None but sullen fools
Castigated canon nought,
Veritable vineyards of novel
New prayer, opened chasms
As deep as Middle Eastern
Oil's layer, luminating
Centuries veins buried deep,
Certifying clearly, noble
Nicene's brave creed, calming
Christian's tired trying and
Nullifying fear, making
Insistent invitations, to

Try bearing near – Try?

Christopher Nolan (Age 14), 1980

LEARN THE HARD WAY

'Scarper you lot,' Big Tom ordered as he saw the police patrol car entering the street. He was in fact leading the retreat. Tom, a fourteen-year-old curly headed lad, was the leader of the small 'Gang'. He was not elected to that position. It was just that he had elected himself and no one would stand up to him.

We ran until our lungs ached for air. Although no one seemed to be following us, something urged us to keep on running. Finally I drew to a halt, I could run no more. It was as if I was about to burst. 'That was a lucky escape,' I announced breathlessly.

Tom stopped close to me. 'It was nothing really,' he answered, trying to act as if he was not at all breathless. 'We outran them easy,' he boasted.

I wished that I could have agreed with him, but my intestines felt as if they had tied themselves into knots and were preventing me from speaking. I looked around. The gang had reassembled itself. Well, at least, all four members had.

'How much did we get?' Jack asked, looking down as Tom emptied the money from the bag he was carrying. The money tingled as it hit the old timber floorboards of the hut we used as a hideout. Tom began to arrange the money, pennies in one pile, silver in another, carefully counting each and every coin. 'Two pounds twenty-four pence,' Tom announced triumphantly after the count. 'Not bad considering we done that booth ten days back,' he added.

The sum of two pounds twenty-four pence seemed to make the crime worthwhile. After all, it was hardly likely that the country would collapse over such a small amount, I told myself. As usual after such a daring escapade dreams of becoming a renowned gangster spread through our heads, but Tom's voice brought us back to our senses.

'If I give you all fifty pence each then that should be about fair,' Tom said, handing out the cash. We knew that this meant that Tom had more than us, but no one dared object. 'Meet here next Wednesday, telephone in Victoria Street is full, should make quite a bit on this one.' Tom related the next plan.

'We'll get caught one of these times,' Clive, the fourth member of the gang, warned us, almost with fear in his voice.

We all turned on him, calling him a coward and other names, but we all knew he was no coward and Clive had more to lose than any of us if we did happen to get caught. His old man would knock him to death. He was a hell of a man.

When I returned home it was past ten o'clock. My parents were sat in the sitting room watching the television, but as I entered I heard the springs on my father's armchair creak as he stood to greet me. 'And what time do you call this?' he said angrily. It was obvious that he had been at the bottle.

'Anything to eat, Mum? I am starving,' I asked my mother, ignoring my father's threat.

My mother rose to make me some supper, but my father pushed her back down. 'You ain't making him any supper,' he warned her. 'Now you listen to me boy, no fourteen-year-old son of mine stays out this late. Where have you been?' He unfastened his belt as a warning.

I continued to ignore him. I placed the kettle on the stove, then searching through the larder, found a full packet of biscuits to fill my empty stomach.

My father stood in the door, his belt hung in his hand, treating me as if I was still a child. 'Where have you been?' he asked again, waiting impatiently for a reply.

'Oh,' I replied, mocking my father to his face. My thrashing days were over, past. I knew that underneath he was more frightened of me than I was of him. My father, due to drinking and smoking and the type of work he did, was a ruined man.

'You have been with that Tom Barrett again. I have told you to keep away from him. He is a bad influence.' My father warned me as he always did in the past, his finger waving at me in anger for disobeying his advice every time.

'Go to hell,' was my reply to this warning. I knew he was only trying to help me, but I hated parents that tried to choose one's friends. The kettle had boiled. I made some coffee and sat waiting for the old man to lose his temper.

'Don't say that to me. If I was your age and said that to my father he would have thrashed the living daylights out of me,' my father said almost red with temper.

'Well, you ain't your father, are you,' I turned on him spitefully. With him it was always what his father would have done if I had been his son, but he was not his father and I, as spitefully and as often as I could, would never let him forget.

The old man swore at me bitterly. Anything said against his father was sacrilege, even though when his father was alive the two men could not stand one another; perhaps the protection of his father was the admission of guilt. 'You will end up in serious trouble one of these days,' he warned.

I pushed past him. He continued to swear at me as I made my way upstairs with the rest of the biscuits. I listened to him as he made his way back to the company of the television, then everything downstairs fell quiet. It was nearly midnight when the doorbell went. My father, who was still up, answered the door, complaining about the lateness of the call.

'Have you got a telephone?' the man asked breathlessly. I could tell by his voice that he was in a panic. Then before my father was able to speak, he continued. 'I must get a doctor, my daughter has had an asthma attack, she could die.' His voice reached a peak.

'There is a telephone on the corner of the street,' my old man told him with no compassion in his voice.

'Out of order. Those damn vandals have been at it again. Please you must help, we need a doctor urgently, my daughter's life is at stake,' the man begged. It was sad to hear him.

'Sorry, we have no phone, but there is one at the end of Victoria Street, about a quarter of a mile away,' my father told him, closing the door. I heard the man's footsteps fade away.

I found it difficult to sleep that night. I regretted not getting up and running to the other phone myself. It was purely a selfish feeling that stopped me, my own comfort.

Next day I was determined to find out what happened to the girl and in some way offer my services to pay back any suffering she may have endured at my expense.

My father sat down to tea next day in his usual impatient way.

135

'That man who was here last night asking if we had a phone, his daughter died before they reached a doctor, at least that is what Jack said. He knew the family,' he announced without any feelings.

'How awful,' added my mother, serving out the food from a big container. It was stew again.

'Bloody vandals, she might have lived had they not ruined the kiosk,' my father added bitterly, looking at me.

I found it difficult to eat my meal, choking almost with every mouthful. I was surprised that no one made any comment. All the time I could feel my father watching me, but not once did I look up at him. After tea I went to my room; all the while my conscience called me a murderer, it was me who killed that girl. I stayed in my room all evening almost too scared to go downstairs. Suddenly my mother stood at the bedroom door with a hot drink.

'Not going out tonight?' she asked, handing me the drink. She still considered me as a child to be nursed even though my father continually rebuked her. I shook my head. 'Sad about that young girl, she was only twelve,' my mother muttered.

I nodded, praying hard that she would drop the subject and go back downstairs leaving me alone again.

'Promise you won't annoy your father so much, you know it only upsets him?' she begged. The expression on her face portrayed one of worry and anxiety.

Like a fool I agreed to her demand. Not for my father's sake, but for my mother's peace of mind, plus the fact that I hoped she would go downstairs and leave me alone, to the effect my prayer was not in vain. I tried to sleep, but my conscience weighed even more heavy than before, even though there was nothing I could do to help the girl.

After some discreet questioning I finally found out where Linda – I had established that that was the unfortunate girl's name – was being buried and the name of the church. Although the thought of attending a funeral did not appeal to me, and by missing school for the afternoon I invited the wrath of the headmaster, I decided to go. Standing a little away from the graveside I watched as the coffin was lowered, never to be seen again. Just a gravestone to commemorate the poor creature. No one noticed me. The grief-stricken family was led away by a weeping father. Although it was a horrible sight I was glad I came.

I arrived back at school just as it was closing for the night. I needed to collect some books so without being noticed I made my way to my classroom, but I knew before I reached there that there would be a reception committee waiting for me.

My prediction was correct; my classteacher sat in her desk, waiting to pounce on her unfortunate victim. 'I thought you would come back, I hear that you have been missing from class all afternoon. Where have you been?' she asked, staring at me over her glasses.

I said nothing but walked slowly to the back of the classroom and stood by my desk in total silence; there was nothing I had to say to her. It was useless to question me.

'Were you ill or something?' was her next question; she was trying to false me in a verbal answer. I shook my head. 'What did you have this afternoon?' she said, studying my timetable. 'Physical Education, I thought you liked that,' she said.

'I do,' I answered, then receded back into my shell, regretting making my reply to her questions.

'Then why did you miss it today? I have never known you to abscond before. It is not like you.' She continued to press me for the reason for my strange disappearance.

I kept my peace. I had absconded before, but always made an alibi for myself. This time I was not going to give the real reason and it was no use lying.

'You know what the punishment is for deliberately staying from classes?' She tried to pressure me to answer.

I nodded, I knew the penalty.

I was led down the dimly lit corridor passing classrooms where cleaners swept pathetically with their brooms knowing that the very next day things would be as untidy as they were today. We finally reached a door where, marked in gold, was the word 'Headmaster'. We entered. He excused the teacher and then began to question me about my whereabouts this afternoon, but received exactly the same answer as my teacher. He flew into a rage. 'Probably up to one of those boyish tricks again, uh?' he said angrily as he took one cane from his desk. The pain was not great; in fact, it seemed as if God was retaliating for the death of the girl. I said nothing.

137

As usual after a caning, there were the obvious questions asked at home, but I gave no clue as to the reason. My father, like the headmaster, flew into a temper at my dismissal of his questions. He, in his normal manner, threatened me with his belt but it was no use . . . 'It wouldn't surprise me if you had something to do with the smashing of the telephone down the road. The police are beginning to ask questions,' my father said.

I said nothing in my defence, the conversation was dropped, and I, with a deep sigh of relief, retired to my room.

Three days passed by, I did not go out in the evening. The thought of meeting the police and being questioned by them scared me. I was afraid of giving some clue away. I had no idea of the consequences, so I took no chances.

Tuesday came, the day of the next escapade. The whole thing had slipped my mind until Jack arrived at the door to enquire if I was coming or not. 'We thought you had got cold feet or something when you failed to turn up,' Jack said as we made our way to the meeting place. I smiled.

Big Tom and Clive were already waiting for me. They greeted me with the usual gang salute, but I did not return the acknowledgment. 'This is the plan,' Tom began, taking a drawn map of the area around the kiosk in Victoria Street from his pocket. 'Now, Clive will keep watch here,' Tom pointed to a spot on the map, 'Jack will be there, while me and you do the tele . . .'

'I ain't going,' I suddenly told them, relieved that I had broken the ice; I had never felt so scared as I did then.

'What do you mean, you ain't going? It's all arranged, you haven't got cold feet have you?' Big Tom said, mocking me.

'No, I have not got cold feet,' I replied in a brave tone. I went on to explain about Linda, and how due to our stupidity, a young girl was lying in the local churchyard. Clive and Jack listened sympathetically to my story, but Tom laughed at my weakness.

'You have gone soft,' he told me harshly, then turned to the others. 'Come on, we will do it without him, he's just yella,' Tom said, leading the group.

Clive and Jack stood still looking from Tom to me and back to me as they tried to make their decision who to follow.

'Come on,' Tom urged, 'think of all that cash, and split three ways, too.' He sounded very persuasive.

Clive turned away. 'Better go or me dad will be looking for me,' he said, leaving.

Jack followed likewise.

Raymond Patrick Bunce, 1976

FIRST LIGHT OF DAWN

Lingering for a moment, like the final chord of a concerto before the explosion of unmistakably spontaneous applause, sleep gave way to a turmoil of mental activity. This waking came gently and smilingly, and it was the cause of it which filled her with the strange mixture of serenity and joy which made memories come flooding into her mind. It was as though she had got a good seat in a box at the theatre, where she could be a spectator in comfort and solitude, but had no power to order the scenes she was reliving; they were history, and no amount of rewriting could change things.

Ever since she was a small child the transition between sleep and wakefulness had frequently been memorably unpleasant; some vivid dreams were still clear in her memory. So often the physical jolt from the world of dreaming to the world of sane reality had rejected the mental jolt, so that the horrors of the fantasy world refused to stay behind, and became frighteningly possible and real. And at other times there had been the feverish struggles to identify a nagging, niggling annoyance in the fantasy world as an actual physical or mental discomfort – a dry throat, the subconscious panic before an exam – which could soon be calmed when rationality returned. But this waking was different: it typified and personified her feeling that there was light ahead and that the darkness was behind her – the night was going, and day was breaking, full of new and unknown things – and full of hope.

It had been his arm falling without his knowing across her body as he stirred in his dreams that had broken her own sleep. She felt glad that he was there, glad that he was touching her – even though he was unaware of it – and glad that they had a future together. Almost overnight she had realised and achieved her ambition: to love and to be loved. So often that question, 'What is your ambition?' had been asked, in the expectancy of some high-powered reply, and so many times she had declined to commit herself, insisting that she was unambitious; and now there was room for new ambitions, spoken or secret. She lay awake in the pressing, whistling silence of the night, and he lay beside her – perhaps with her in his dreams, perhaps far away. It was strange that she could be so close to another human being, and yet her thoughts could be her own. She welcomed this undisturbed opportunity to remember: to be private and yet have companionship.

She could not recall ever worrying about her eyes herself, and yet on reflection she was certain that her parents must have spent many agonising hours waiting for the results of the latest eye surgery to be manifested. Those awful words, 'Go with nurse, while I have a talk with Mummy', had always meant the same thing – another attempt to save her sight a little longer; but at the time it had just meant another stay in hospital, with more injections to fear to the point of panicky crying. Nurses had always been kind: chatting, giving her sweets and syringes to play with, letting her push the tea-trolleys. And then Mummy had emerged, and announced the already known and accepted verdict: another operation. Floods of tears would follow, soon turned to smiles by a large chocolate ice-cream in a restaurant on Regent Street, and the injections would fade away. To her the visits to the hospital had simply meant more injections, but to her parents they had meant another step along the road towards the inevitable loss of all sight. How small her childish worries seemed when compared with those of her parents; and yet then they had been so mammoth and vitally important.

Memories of her sight deteriorating were very blurred; it happened quickly when it came, and she could clearly remember staring at a page of writing which just looked like a fuzzy blur, unable to distinguish even the lines of print. And then that last visit to the surgeon, and going out with nurse while Mummy was talked to. But this time Mummy didn't come out within minutes, and the anxiety grew in her. She had already accepted that this meant another operation, but why was Mummy so long? Nurse had given her a yellow rose on that occasion, and she had feverishly picked it to bits while she cried, sensing the potency of the occasion. It seemed like ages before Mummy had come, and she looked grey and miserable when she did appear. It was she who had said, 'You must stay in hospital now and have an operation, and you won't be able to see any more when you wake up.' She had said it so sadly and gently. Even then, the injections had been the menace, not the loss of sight: she could remember asking if she would still be able to draw when she couldn't see – so Mummy suggested she look the other way and try, and she did a doodle which pleased her. To a seven-year-old the prospect of not being able to see was of no meaning or consequence; it wasn't a thing to fear, just a new idea, which made it like an exciting new game.

The day after the dissection of the martyred yellow rose, she had made her first Holy Communion. Everyone was there, everyone was kind, and she was excited with the attention she received, the presents, and the awesome occasion. There was no fear at all – just the excitement of showing the white heart-shaped rosary beads to the other eye patients when visiting time was over, and the little white book with the cross on the front. The day that her parents must still remember so well had no memories for her – the day that her eye was relieved of its faulty duties for ever. Far more memorable was the first walk without sight: taking some strawberries, which were a present for a little girl in hospital, to the kitchens with no one holding her hand. And it had been easy.

Then the new and very different life had begun. There was the excitement of learning to read again – but this time in Braille – and going to boarding school. Because she was reasonably intelligent, she had soon made up lost ground, and caught up with the others academically. But she had not been happy all the time. It seemed crystal clear to her now, thinking back, that she must have been psychologically very disturbed over her loss of sight as a primary-school child, although she had not recognised that at the time. She could clearly recall doing diabolical crimes of bullying, and sometimes lying awake at night, crying and praying almost hysterically, and begging God to let her see again, to make the angels come and make the darkness go away. She clearly remembered straining her eyes, willing them to see even light, and being frustrated with herself and God when she couldn't. And yet she could remember many more times when she had been very happy: see-sawing for hours on end, having midnight feasts at about ten at night which were so exciting, going for donkey rides, and climbing trees.

Then there had been secondary school. There she had grown bitter about not being able to see, and had learnt the worst aspect of it: the inability and unwillingness of some seeing people to accept her and treat her as a normal teenager, with the same aspirations and idiocies as other girls of her age who could see. She had gone through the painful stage of rejecting all help, and trying to manage without her white stick, finding any indication of her blindness repugnant.

That school had worked marvels for her academically, and made her a nicer, more caring, less bullying person, but socially she had become frustrated: there was very little opportunity to meet people, especially boys, and when such rare occasions did happen, lack of experience and the desire to impress had been disastrous: she had plastered her face with make-up, worn out-landish and unsuitable clothes, and generally made a fool of herself.

The three school dances, one a year from the fourth form, stood out clearly in her memory even now: she had longed each time to find a boyfriend, and had failed each time. She and her friends had to fantasise, and often this led to deep depression; this contagious disease would engulf them all, so that she could remember despairing of ever being considered as a normal girl, with normal desires. It was so easy now, looking back on those unhappy times, to feel pitying amusement – so very easy now that she could reach out and touch the person who could and did give her love. It seemed to be the pattern of her life, and probably of many other people's lives: things were so vitally important at the time, worries so real and insurmountable, and yet when you looked back from the other side, they seemed trivial and pathetic.

She had always been one of the lucky ones: she had not worked in the sixth form, but had just managed to haul herself through A-Levels at sufficient standards to meet university entry condi-tions.

And then, one by one, the bad things began to fade away. She learnt to accept her lack of sight, and to try and be efficient and blind rather than pretending not to be blind and being inefficient. So much depended on attitude, her own and other people's; she knew her own attitude towards herself had been wrong, and once she altered that, other people were more able to alter their attitudes towards her.

Having secured a university place, she decided, a decision she had never regretted, to spend a year living at home and working. She had done one of the things that had vastly changed her life then, training with a guide dog. Her dog had brought her independence she never realised was within reach, and it had brought her friends. And after the year, she had packed up her things, and set off for a new experience at university. She had experienced huge fears and apprehensions at broaching this new world, in which she would be so much alone.

She could distinctly remember waving goodbye to her parents, and a feeling of unbelievable loneliness sweeping through her whole body. She had realised in a split second that she must either pull herself together and make friends, or be left behind like a helpless vegetable. It had taken a lot of steeling up, but she had gone and banged on doors, introduced herself, and received mixed receptions, but she'd broken the ice with a few people – and although she was 'not quite ordinary' she had been accepted, to her delight.

And then, with the new year, had come the fulfilment of the unspoken ambition, the arrival of the body and soul that lay peacefully beside her now. And that first year had been the happiest of her non-childhood. For he was different; he understood from the first that she shared the same hopes and fears, desires and love, as other girls. It did not matter to him that there were things she could not do, or found difficult, that her eyes looked strange, that people stared at her sometimes. He loved her because she was herself, and he wanted to share his life with her.

And now she lay in the stillness, and knew for certain that everything from the past had been worth it. As strongly and bound to be noticed as the smell of freshly roasted coffee beans, the thought came to her that she had always been destined to be happy: her parents had managed to turn their tragedy into her joy by treating her normally, and making her feel this to be important. She didn't need to feel unordinary at home, because she was just one of the family. And now she had found someone else who felt the same about her – someone who wanted to, and would, be part of her new family. It would be ludicrous to imagine or pretend that the future would all be rosy: but then, surely, that was what living was all about – you strived for good results, and experienced enormous joy and a sense of satisfaction when such were achieved.

Then, as the warm feeling of tiredness and intense joy flowed over her body, like the ripples of the breeze on a burning summer day, she turned on to her side, cuddled into his chest, and thanked God for sending his angels to take away the darkness.

Claire Wheeler, 1977

THE TIME WILL COME

The school was strangely silent now, the last echoes of laughter fading as the children made their way across the playground. Their joy and excitement were evident to even the most casual of observers. Yes the end of term concert had been a great success. I smiled pensively as I watched the last of the children pass through the school gates, holding their parent's hand or skipping gaily at their side.

The girls' long dresses and paper bonnets ruffled gently in the slight July breeze. For an evening they had been Victorian ladies and relished every moment of it while the boys had become men lording it over their women complete with mufflers, waistcoats, snuff boxes and dandelion and burdock 'beer'. All had played their part well and I too had played my part. I had smiled and laughed in the right places, striving to hide the hollowness within. The children had been proud to show me off to their parents, after all it's not everyone who has a dalek for a teacher! To give them their due, the parents seemed suitably impressed with the batteries and electronic hardware of my wheelchair. There had been no hint of reservation about their child being taught by a disabled teacher. Not that it mattered now, it was over, my teaching practice was at an end. The words of the Principal echoed in my ears: 'No one is doubting your ability to teach, we're all agreed you are a very good teacher and you manage very well considering your handicap, but we cannot grant you a teaching certificate. The regulations don't allow us to do so. You haven't failed the course, you understand, it's just we can't allow you to teach.'

The hopes and efforts of a lifetime had been shattered in that moment. Not able to teach? Not able to drive around the classroom checking their books? Not to buzz down the corridor like an electronic bumble bee? No, surely they couldn't mean that?

146

But the nightmare had gone on; I had travelled the path from the Principal's office to the college entrance without anyone calling, 'Come back, it's a mistake.'

It was true. I had returned to 'my school' for the last time. The concert to which we had all looked forward for so long had become for me a punctuation mark in an episode of despair. My dream was over. As if to emphasise the pain, displayed around the room were the products of the last few weeks' work. The lino-cuts and hand prints, what a messy lesson that had been! The bar-graphs from the maths session on weight, poor Emma had done well to survive the teasing of her slimmer classmates. There was the display of slate paintings, how they had enjoyed themselves that day, sandpapering and decorating their pieces. No doubt we had contravened a law or two on health and safety but the results were remarkable. Especially for Jamie, at last he had found something he could do well, a medium in which he could express himself, no longer bound by the conventional tools of words and paper which for him held no meaning and had become objects of rejection. Oh the frustration of having to leave him just when a promising relationship was developing! True Wendy would take over again – she was a fine teacher and I could not have stayed even if allowed to qualify. But there might have been other Jamies whom I could have taught – other children with whom I could have developed a special relationship because we both have problems in doing what other people accomplish with ease. These were the children with whom I so desperately wanted to work; the not-so-goods and the downright 'thickos', the ones most teachers prefer not to have because they usually disrupt when they fail to construct. It was with such children in mind that I studied psychology at university and fought for a place at teacher training college. Now all these noble intentions were not to be. Legislation had beaten me in the end.

I looked down at the roses and greeting cards lying on my desk. Each card had been carefully decorated and sometimes, laboriously signed: 'To Miss with love', 'To our bionic teacher', and so on. The heady perfume of the roses drifted gently to my nostrils. I breathed in deeply, closing my eyes for a moment in an effort to block out the events of the day. A sudden noise startled me from my introspection, the classroom door swung open as Wayne burst in, looking, as always, like the Artful Dodger. Breathless he exclaimed, 'Oh Miss, I d'nt think I'd catch yer, I thought y'd gone.'

'No, not yet. I'm just collecting my things and having a last look around.'

'I-I j-just wanted to give yer this,' and he unceremoniously pushed a somewhat crumpled blue rose into my lap. 'It ain't much I know, but me mom d'nt gimme any pocket money this week,' and he rubbed his sleeve across his face. I noticed another button was missing from his shirt and there was no lace in his left shoe.

'Oh Wayne, it's beautiful but wherever did you get a blue rose? It's most unusual.'

'Me – er Gran grows 'em, 'er's got lots,' he stuttered, shuffling from one foot to the other as he always did when being not altogether truthful.

'She must have a big window box in her flat,' I commented, trying to sound deceived.

'Oh 'er 'as – it's enormous Miss,' he said, relaxing at the sudden and surprising gullibility of the teacher with whom he had had more than one disagreement. Now was not the time to adopt my professional role.

'I shall put your flower in the middle of my rose bowl at home together with those the other children have given me.'

'There ain't nobody else give yer a blue rose 'as there, Miss? I did want t' give yer somat special like. I thought it 'ud match yer dress. I bought a pin to stick it on with,' and he pulled an enormous rusty safety pin out of his pocket.

'Yes, you're right Wayne, it will match my dress. Help me pin it on, will you please?' Together we attached the now weary looking rose to my lapel. I tried not to think about the two holes and the brown stain which the ancient pin would leave in the cotton dress.

'What school am yer going to next Miss?' asked Wayne, running his hands across a pile of text books. The question cut deep.

'I'm not going to another school, Wayne, the people in charge say I can't teach any more because I can't walk.'

'But you've got yer electric thingy – it's ever so fast. I wish I had one,' and he came close to me, gazing in sheer delight at the control box.

'Yes, I know, but the people who decide who can become a teacher think I can't teach you properly if I can't walk.'

'That's daft,' he exclaimed, holding his hand an inch or two above the control knob and looking to see if I had noticed.

I looked at his grubby face and clear blue eyes, desperately trying to resist the urge to flatten the strands of hair which stuck out just above his left ear. Junior teachers do not mother their pupils I reminded myself.

'Oh Miss, I ain't 'alf going to miss yer!' and he flung his arms around me in a rib cracking squeeze. The classroom went a little misty.

The door opened quietly and John entered the room. Our eyes met across the top of the child's head. Understanding the sanctity of the moment he tip-toed into the corner and perched on the draining board. Wayne took two paces from me and half turned to see who had entered. His face coloured a little on seeing we were observed. He coughed, rubbed his arm across his face again and said lightly, 'Well, I'm going now, Miss, me mom said to meet 'er outside the boozer at nine.'

'It's almost that now.'

'Ar, Miss,' he agreed.

'Bye Wayne, and thanks for the rose.'

'That's all right, Miss. Bye,' and ran off down the corridor before he had the chance to say or do anything else 'soppy'.

John walked towards me. 'I thought he was one of the unmanageables?'

'He is,' I said sardonically.

John gathered my things up from the desk. 'Ready to go?'

I nodded.

'Has it been very hard?' he asked, looking me straight in the eye.

I looked down at my blue rose, unable to meet his gaze, 'Pretty bad.'

'Well, don't let Mr Haynes see you with that or it'll be even worse. Somebody's just stolen it from his garden and it was his pride and joy.'

The truth dawned. Wayne had helped himself from the caretaker's garden. Perhaps it was as well it was my last day. I slipped the evidence into my handbag, feeling like a partner in crime.

John walked towards the door and reached for the light switch.

I moved the wheelchair towards him. The classroom shrank into shadow as the light went out. The red glow from the light on the wheelchair gave the room a pink glow. The tyres squelched on the wooden floor as I turned to take a last look. I relived once more the good days and the bad days I had known in that classroom. The worry when it seemed they would never settle down, the deep joy of the precious times I knew that I held the children's attention totally. The laughter (despite myself) at some of Simon's antics, the feeling of inadequacy when Lucy's mother died unexpectedly. Now it was over, never again would I know such moments. In utter frustration I beat my fists on the arm of my wheelchair.

'Oh, why can't they understand, I *can* help these kids, I *can* teach them, I know I can! When will they see all the things I can do instead of looking at the few I can't? *Why* are they so blind? Disability is *not* the same as debility! I *did* so want to teach, I really *did*!'

Two hot, angry tears spilled, unchecked on to my cheeks, hiding in the shadow of the classroom. For a moment there was complete silence broken only by the occasional 'plop' from the leaky tap over the sink. Mr Haynes had never repaired it.

John moved slowly and deliberately towards me, his face unnaturally rosy in the glow of my light. He knelt down, taking me firmly by the shoulders. I looked searchingly into his eyes.

'You can teach and you've got a lot to offer these kids. And the time will come when they'll realise what you *can* do and that there *are* ways to get round what you can't manage. One day someone will be brave enough to say, "Go ahead, we'll risk it," and they'll find out that you and others like you, weren't a risk at all. It'll happen – be sure of that – the time *will* come.'

I sighed deeply – words were beyond me now. He was probably right. But when would that time come?

Hilary Stevenson, 1980

OH 'L' IT'S OWEN

On reflection, it seems fair to say that my relationship with the medical profession, especially the Orthopaedic section, has been far from harmonious.

Therefore when, at the age of thirteen, I was told that I would never be able to drive, my feelings were a mixture of adolescent disappointment and gross anger, although not surprise, as this was a statement of stupidity at which they were expert.

Twenty-two years later, a chance meeting between my mother and an old friend of mine from The Spastics Society, brought a change of fortune for me. During a lunchtime conversation Mother said that the one thing which still annoyed me was the fact of not being able to drive.

Now, one of the numerous virtues which The Spastics Society possesses is the ability to ignore negative statements, such as: 'impossible', 'never', or the favourite one of all, 'can't'. Instead, they adopt a positive approach by taking endless time and care to find out exactly what an individual spastic *can* do.

Naturally this is a marvellous help to an individual like myself, who has no wish to be an exhibitionist, but merely someone constantly striving to make my disability as unimportant as possible.

My friend, Ann Hithersay, knowing me well as a pretty capable sort of chap, with a positive outlook on life, was rather amazed to learn that I had been put off the idea of driving by white-coated bureaucracy and promised to obtain some help and advice on this matter.

A mere two months passed and I received a letter from the Head of the British School of Motoring, inviting me to their offices in Chelsea for a driving assessment.

On arrival, Mother and I were met by Mr Barker who was one of the top Assessment Officers for BSM's Disabled Drivers

Department; although he was one of the most charming people I had ever met, I was quickly and firmly told that his job was not just to satisfy my ambition but to ensure that I was capable of driving safely.

Just to prove his point, Mr Barker put me through forty minutes of intense physical and mental pressure on an Assimulator, which is a shell of normal car with all the appropriate pedals, gears and instrument panel, the only difference being that it does not move, which is a great idea especially for an idiot like me, who had never even sat behind the steering wheel.

After this slightly strenuous ordeal, Mr Barker looked over the top of his spectacles. 'Right, young sir, you will drive, but before I complete my report I want you to go home, get a Provisional Licence, then return here so that I can take you out on the road.' At this point I smiled broadly, but poor Mum turned a whiter shade of pale.

Four months later, I was back in Chelsea with Mr Barker; however, this time I had Mum and Dad with me. Obviously they had decided that if I killed myself it would take the two of them to bring the coffin home on the train.

From his assessment of my previous visit, Mr Barker had decided that I would only be able to drive an automatic car; unfortunately, the two automatic metros which the BSM had in their Chelsea branch were out on tuition, therefore I had to use Mr Barker's own car for my first drive.

My parents remained in the office while Mr Barker and I went around to the garage at the rear. As we entered he pointed to a large red Triumph 2000. 'This is it, now I'll take it out for five minutes while you watch my every movement. Any questions?' I didn't reply, I just thought, if I'm going to drive I might as well start in a big way.

Those five minutes just flew and before I knew it, there I was behind the wheel, belted up and ready for off; it was truly a marvellous sensation as I started the engine, put the gear into 'drive' and moved away. After crawling up and down some back roads, Mr Barker chucked me in at the deep end by ordering me to turn left suddenly. I found myself facing a massive roundabout; he casually told me to wait for a gap in the traffic and take exit four which led into King's Road.

With suicidal boldness I made for a small gap, then completed three circuits of that roundabout, wedged between a laundry van and a lorry carrying toilet rolls. Eventually the van driver got tired of fooling around and turned off; this gave me the chance to see where I was going and take exit four, down King's Road and back to BSM's office.

After a few minutes of welcome silence, Mr Barker turned and beamed, 'You'll do mate, anyone who can stay cool under those conditions has a ninety per cent chance of becoming a good driver. By the way, does anything make you panic?'

My regular tuition began in Swansea during May 1982, in a BSM metro which had been adapted to suit the needs of every disabled pupil in Wales. Unfortunately for me, the car and the specially trained instructor were based in Newport; this meant that I always had my lesson bang in the middle of the lunch hour traffic.

For the initial four lessons my instructor was Silent Sid, an old gent who just sat beside me and smoked one cigarette after another; he didn't actually instruct me, but merely told me which way to go.

Some may think this rather odd, but I reckon old Sid was a wise old fox; instead of cramming my brain with facts, he just allowed me to get the 'feel' of the car. However, he didn't take me on any quiet roads, because that is not BSM policy, but through as much heavy traffic as possible; this is a good idea because it certainly keeps your concentration and reactions sharp.

The day before my fifth lesson BSM informed me that the metro had broken down and that Silent Sid was in poor shape also. In actual fact he was finding the increase in work load a bit much and had decided to retire. Mind you, I'm sure he was a little shaken the previous week when my foot brake failed on Glanmor Hill; no need for him to flap, I just put it into 'neutral' gear and it stopped.

My next instructor was totally different; he was just thirty and had been trained by Mr Barker, which meant that although he was a super guy to work with he allowed me no room for errors. I knew that each time I made a mistake with Clive, he'd make me go back and do it again and again. Although this was tougher, it was rewarding, as he showed great faith in my ability, which in turn made me try even harder.

Then Clive became ambitious and introduced me to the joys of reversing around corners and three-point turns. Funny thing about reversing, the car and I seemed to go our separate ways; as for the three-point turn, after going backwards and forwards across a busy road, my poor brain became disorientated.

At this stage, I should make it clear that each two hour lesson was not entirely spent in a moronic atmosphere; for one thing it's quite impossible for me to remain in a serious frame of mind on any occasion for over thirty minutes.

It constantly appears to me that 'humour' is either misused or undervalued. After all, if I approached each driving lesson in a 'life or death' manner, I would become physically and mentally 'uptight' and that's when the element of doubt about your ability will creep in, destroying the self-confidence which is so vital.

Two examples of how my humour freed me from two potentially dangerous situations. Firstly, take a foggy morning outside a Chapel of Rest, where I was on the very brink of doing a three-point turn in three; now I had gone forward with precision, then went back with luck, just as I was about to perform a perfect right turn, the door of the Chapel of Rest flew open and a coffin shot straight out in front of the car.

After slamming on the foot brake, I turned to Clive, who had now got his pen wedged up his right nostril, asking what the . . . was going on? He didn't reply, just sat there looking rather silly. Meanwhile the sound of screaming brakes brought one of the undertaker's staff rushing out; he peered in the car window. 'Don't worry, son, it was empty.' I glared at him and promised, 'When I die, you won't have my custom.'

The other occasion which I found hilarious was the time Clive chose to put my reactions to the test by practising an emergency stop.

According to the Highway Code, which Clive recited with the fluency of a Shakespearian actor, it was illegal to perform an emergency stop in a residential area unless it was justified.

I was told to drive to one of the local industrial estates for this particular act; on route I was also informed that it is essential to stop in under 1.4 seconds in order to reach test standard.

Being a jolly good pupil and twit, I proceeded along this stretch of straight road on the industrial estate at a steady 40 mph; it was a lovely day, the sun shone, the birds sang and the pollen count was doing a great job on my hay fever.

Then it happened. Clive hit the dashboard with his hand, I stopped and all hell broke loose. Now without wishing to appear boastful, I must admit to being rather quick; in fact I was quite proud of my efforts as I sat back, allowing the vertebrae in my neck sufficient time to stop playing musical chairs and return to their normal position.

It was a great shame that poor old Clive's seat-belt wasn't properly locked, because when I stopped, Clive kept going. It's a sad sight, seeing a qualified instructor reduced to a crumpled heap on the floor and his head in the glove compartment.

Ten minutes passed before he was back to normal, although his glasses were slightly bent; fair play, he did eventually praise me, despite the fact that his stopwatch had vanished out of the window.

Meanwhile, my parents and I pooled our resources and bought a gorgeous Datsun automatic in metallic gold, which I'm very proud of. It's smart, large and responsive, a sort of four-wheeled version of Bo Derek.

However, I admit that the first time I drove it I was a little timid, because all I could see was this vast expanse of metallic gold bonnet. It took a while for me to keep it on my side of the road, but after a few weeks I found driving a large car easier than the metro.

Although I was now driving our own car at weekends, I was still having tuition with Clive on the BSM metro. He became rather concerned about my three-point turn, despite the fact that I could now do it in four – well sometimes.

Knowing full well that we had just bought a new car, he came up with the idea that we should now change it for one with power assisted steering, which would make every type of turn completely effortless; after finding out that it would have cost at least £1,500 to have this adaptation, my parents and I went off the idea rather quickly.

By Christmas, Clive had become totally obsessed by his idea, to the point whereby whatever I did right, he would always say, 'But you'd do that far better with power steering.' After a while this became a little annoying, so my parents and I decided to give Clive the elbow for a few months and concentrate on driving our car; after all, a little more effort doesn't cost anything. Besides, *motivation* will leave *power steering* standing any day.

Therefore, every weekend since January, my father has been giving me tuition. At this point I must publicly offer my sincere gratitude to my father, because he is an excellent teacher and so far we've not had a cross word – occasionally he shouts but that is only to keep my concentration on the ball.

As regards taking my driving test, I have not fixed a definite date simply because there are still a few flaws to be ironed out, which I fully recognise and admit to. Besides I want to be sure I pass first time; anything less will be an anticlimax and make all my efforts completely abortive.

At present, I find driving an extremely enjoyable and very challenging experience; having said that, I'm still furious with those certain people who stated I couldn't drive.

Obviously everyone is vulnerable to errors of judgment; however, when such mistakes can seriously affect an individual's lifestyle, then more thought and less talk would be beneficial.

Furthermore, I flatly refuse to allow my parents to take any blame; as always they were only seeking the best possible advice, totally unaware of the suppressive attitude which the medical profession has towards spasticity.

After all, being without mobility for twenty-two years has made social life with people of my own age virtually impossible, plus blotting out any hope of an intimate relationship with the opposite sex.

Oh, I fully realise that the 'average' disabled person is not supposed to have such aspirations; on the other hand, who the devil wants to be average?

Owen Davies, 1983

THE SEASONS

AUTUMN

In the Autumn the
Leaves fall,
At night we hear the
Owls call.
The Squirrels call to
the trees,
gathering nuts as
they please.

Matthew Barber (Age 9), 1979

SEASONS

The world is a dazzling white
Twists of smoke rising from brick chimneys
Sounds of high pitched shouts and laughter
Young people skating on an ice-covered pond
A log fire dancing in a cosy sitting room
The swish of smooth velvet curtains being drawn
The cosiness of the dim-lit room.
Morning breaks, a shaft of sunlight
Melting icicles, a blade of grass
Appears through the soft white sheet
Of thawing snow, now melting
Into the rich moist earth.
A patch of hazy blue sky
The first delicate flower
Displaying its splash of colour
The sweet smell of freshly cut grass
A child sitting on a lawn
Idly making daisies into chains
The once naked trees have new life
A lamb bleating for its mother
Dust rising from the scorched ground
The bubbling stream
The heat of the blazing sun
Then, the refreshing sound of rain
Upon the dry wrinkled leaves
A strong gust of wind whistles
Through the bare withered trees
These are some of the beauties
We often take for granted.

Ann Grange (Age 15), 1982

A POEM OF SPRING

In Spring it is nice and warm,
The birds sing merrily at dawn,
The days are getting longer
The animals awake,
And squirrels jump about the trees,
And daffodils are by the lake.

I look forward to the brighter days,
Because I can go out and play,
I do not have to stay indoors
I can ride my bike for hours and hours
And be outdoors, in Aston Park
On the bright green grass and spring flowers.

My mother's busy in the house,
She puts new curtains up,
They're white and clean and have a sheen
And the sun shines through the house.

Chris Givans (Age 12), 1980

SNOWFLAKES

Snow, lovely snow,
For lord and lady,
Now and piano,
No longer malady,
Party Maffia,
Amicable map,
Melody on marketry,
Photography all marly,
Aorsan man opens,
Opera play solo,
A god in mephitis;
No melancholy.

CHRISTMAS

Pies of mincemeat,
An ear asleep,
A smell of cooking,
A merry feast.
A meaty turkey,
A roasting aroma,
Apron olagorachy,
A post quota,
A priest at prayer,
A tasselled altar.

TREES ROAN

Naught ought be suggested,
Ulegized, penurized,
Honoured and nurtured,
More orange appearing
Emblazoned, meandering,
Mad red, land brown,
Meadow green,
Mellow yellow,
Are the colours
Of the roan trees.

Christopher Nolan (Age 12), 1978

WHEN SANTA CLAUS COMES

There's a snowflake on the window
And a nightlight by my head,
There's a moonbeam on the pillow
And a stocking on the bed.

There's a bell upon the steeple
And a carol in the street,
There's a turkey in the pantry
And a stocking by my feet.

There's a silence in the bedroom
And a mystery in the air,
And there's something going to happen
For my stocking's hanging there.

There's a tiptoe on the stairs
Santa Claus, I really do believe,
But I'm going to shut my eyes
For you must on Christmas eve.

Olwyn Northey, 1971

THE AULD YEAR'S NIGHT STORY

One Auld Year's night, we were sitting round the muckle fire. The clock on the mantelpiece showed eleven. Mum and Gran were sitting knitting jerseys, Dad was sleeping, and Stuart, my brother, was lying on the floor reading. Granpaw and I were just sitting.

Granpaw is bald nowadays, but he used to have fair hair like me. He has a big face, and a wee nose to snore well. He has an old skin with lots of lines, and his eyes are bluey grey like mine. His teeth are false and he wears specs for reading. He's a bit of a comic, and says, 'I'd better get awa' to ma bed,' when he wants you to go hame. (Gran's face goes scarlet red then!)

Well, Granpaw and I were just sitting and I said to him, 'Tell me a story about your teenage.' This is what he told me.

Two months before I left the school, ma mither took me aside and said, 'Me and your faither have been thinking – what about you going to Cupar Market and getting a fee? Yer faither's got the afternoon off to gang wi' ye. I've kept back some clean cla'es for you to put on.'

So I went to Cupar Market wi' ma faither and we roamed about the streets for a while, waiting for a farmer to come up to us. The toon was filled wi' young men waiting for the words, 'You want a fee?' and ready to answer, 'Aye, I am.'

When it was my turn, the farmer said, 'Let me see your character laddie.' The laddies usually had a report from the school. The farmer looked at it. 'That's a guid character. I'll gi'e ye your milk and meal, coals and tatties and thirty shillings a week.'

'Well, laddie, are ye takin' it or no?' said ma faither.

'Oh, aye. When do you want me to start?'

'Start as soon as you leave school. Come awa' now, I'll buy your faither a pint.'

Well, I came hame shouting, 'Mither, I've got a fee for six months, at Broomhall Farm only five miles away. My pay will be a two-pint pitcher of milk a day, a furlett o' meal, free coal and tatties, and thirty bob a week.'

Ma mither said to me, 'Ye ken Bob doon the road? Here's some money. Awa' and buy a kist to yersel' for a' yer cla'es. Ye can pay me back wi' your first pay.'

I went oot singing to masel':

> 'When I was only twal years auld,
> I left the village school.
> Ma faither sent me to the ploo'
> To win ma milk and meal.'

Well, the time was coming roond when I'd to go to the bothy. Ma mither packed ma kist wi' cla'es – Sunday suit and cords for working. School days were over.

For the first two days I enjoyed the work. Nae faither walloping ma lug or sending me to ma bed. Nae mither to say, 'Wipe your feet on the mat.'

Then there came a rainy morning when I got soaked at the plooing and I felt like rinning awa' hame to ma mither. Nae clean cla'es. Nae wee cups o' tea. I felt like rinning awa'. A' that month I felt the same, but I knew if I went hame I'd get a kick up the pants! So I stuck it oot. Then I saw a bonnie wee maid in the kitchen and that helped!

> 'Syne at half-five we follow oor nose,
> Ower tae the kitchie tae chaw oor brose.
> Fairm servants seldom need a dose
> O' caster ile in the morning.'

Now, about brose. You put meal, and a teaspoon of salt in a bowl and add boiling hot water. Ye stir it up wi' a wooden spurtle and it's ready to eat. Grand stuff.

One day the minister came into the bothy where the farm workers lived. The men were all sitting down to their dinner on the big scrubbed table with yesterday's paper for a tablecloth. There were pints on the table too, but they were quickly hidden under the table. Dinner was the same as breakfast and tea – brose.

The minister said, 'Do you never get anything else but porridge!' The Gaffer said, 'We like our meat even if it's only brose.' Then they all sang 'For the beauty of the Earth' while their brose got cold!

I'll tell you mair aboot the bothy though. When I first started, ma bothy mate said, 'I'll tak' the pan-a-week (housekeeping) seeing it's your first week at the bothy. You can do it next week.'

Doing the pan-a-week meant cleaning the ashes out once a week, and also raking up the fireside every day and pushing back the fender. Pan-a-weekers rose at fower o'clock to put on the brose. They went out for coal and water. Then they made the beds from which the other men had risen in their semmets and shirt tails to draw on their working cla'es. There were tatties to peel into the brose pot to leave ready for Jock's wife to put on the fire.

Sometimes there was an egg for tea. The farmer kept hens and the men often took an egg if the hens laid outside. Then they had a boil up in the tea water. The farmer never caught them, or maybe he turned a blind eye!

Inside the bothy the fireplace was high up from the floor – halfway up the wall with a space beneath for the ashes to fall. Bowls were washed out and the dirty water thrown on the ashes. The pot was a roond iron one with a big handle over the top, and the kettle was the same with a spout. Above the fireplace was a gas lamp fixed to the wall. It was made of brass, but the bothy men never cleaned it. There was a glass shade over the flame. On the opposite side of the mantel were pictures of our mithers. We had a food kist in the corner where we kept milk, cheese, meal, bread, jam, butter and our brose bowls.

On a Sunday, I put on ma best suit and went off hame on my pedal bike. I got a motor bike later. Ma first words when I got in were, 'Mither, here's ma dirty washing!' The Sabbath was a grand day for a rest, for the rest of the week was busy on the farm.

At the sowing time we planted barley, wheat and oats. Once there wasn't enough corn to sow the field and so one of the young lads sowed it in bits – and when the corn came up there were bare patches all over the field! The farmer wasn't pleased, I can tell you.

At tattie time, all the men went out with sacks on their backs and hand planted the tatties with one foot pace between each. But in winter it was a thought to go out in the pouring rain to mend farm gates and other odd jobs, I can tell you.

One of the great times of the year was the plooing match. Three months before it the men would be up polishing the harness. They were up all night before the match ready to go out at five o'clock to the cuddy to feed it and groom it. Its tail was plaited and its coat polished till it shone. Then on went the bit and bells and man and horse went off knowing there was the chance of winning a prize and, better still, a chance to meet old cronies.

The prize was a rosette and a certificate. I once won second prize wi' ma horse 'Little' – a great big brown beast. And there was always the chaffing. 'That horse can't touch mine. He'll never get first prize. He can't keep a straight dreel like mine.'

They started plooing two dreels and put the earth up to one side. Then the ploo had to work doon one side and up the other to make a straight line to follow for the rest of the field. The judges looked for the straightest, neatest furrow, and the best looking horse.

Ye want to ken mair aboot that wee kitchen lassie do you? Well, I met up wi' her in the coo-shed. She was at the milking and I was at the dung, and I said, 'What aboot us going oot?'

'I ha'e to be in by eleeven o'clock.'

'Easy!'

We went to the silent movies at Leven and paid a penny to go in and see Charlie Chaplin and have a cuddle in the back row chummy seats!

But that's twelve o'clock striking. Happy New Year. Granpaw had his dram and we all went to our beds.

Granpaw Jim makes me laugh sometimes. He says, 'Right Jim, are ye wanting a skelp on the nose or the lug?' Then he spits on his hands and puts his fists up. He's a grand storyteller too.

Muckle	big
Fee	a job
Furlett	28 lbs
Tatties	potatoes
Kist	wooden trunk
Bothy	unmarried male farm workers' lodging
Walloping	hitting
Lug	ear
Spurtle	a wooden spoon
Semmets	vests
Cronies	friends
Dreel	row
Dram	whisky
Skelp	hit

James Anderson (Age 14), 1978

A DESCRIPTIVE ARTICLE

As I sit on the pebbled wall, picking the pebbles off one by one, the sun beats down upon me without mercy. Drinking the lemonade, I can feel it cold, draining into my stomach. The bubbles prick my throat like little needles. Soon the drink is gone. Relieved by it I go and bask in the sun which has already started to burn me. Going to sunbathe is a good excuse for being lazy. Lazy bees hum to themselves in the complex cones of the roses; their odour drifts like a glider on the soft wind. The shallow cool clear brook runs on into the river. I can hear it singing just above the hum of the bees and flies. The sun just carries on throwing its rays at me, oblivious of what is going on around me. The only sounds I can hear are the bees, the brook, the birds and the drone of the tired aeroplane straining to keep to the skies. No other sound – not even the sound of traffic is brought to me by the slight breeze which seems to keep everything from burning. A flock of pigeons fly to and fro over my head like a squadron of aeroplanes. I can almost feel them blocking out the soft and warm rays of the sun. The birds sound half asleep but they keep on singing. The aeroplane retreats from the sky and goes home to rest. The drone of it fades and disappears completely. A tortoise waddles into the shade and is lost from sight amongst the cool long grass. The dog comes from behind the shade of the wall and creeps to her fast emptying drinking bowl like a man from the desert; she drinks. She creeps as if she dare not make a sound. A few fish jump, and plop back into the water. A faint sound of children playing is lifted and carried on the wind.

I think it must be time to get up and go to have a shower, to feel the cold and smooth fingers feeling their way down my spine; the water sounds like rain hitting the bottom of the bath. The thought of it makes me feel much cooler. I don't think I will get up after all. I will fall asleep to the song of the brook, the birds and the bees.

Steven Simmonds (Age 15), 1979